A12900 578386
D1278191
ILLINOIS CE
PR6023.U24C6 1971x
STACKS
Cloud and silver.
A12900 578386

CLOUD AND SILVER

E. V. L U C A S

CLOUD *and* SILVER

BY

EDWARD V. LUCAS

Essay Index Reprint Series

BOOKS FOR LIBRARIES PRESS
FREEPORT, NEW YORK

First Published 1916
Reprinted 1971

INTERNATIONAL STANDARD BOOK NUMBER:
0-8369-2411-8

LIBRARY OF CONGRESS CATALOG CARD NUMBER:
73-156685

PRINTED IN THE UNITED STATES OF AMERICA
BY
NEW WORLD BOOK MANUFACTURING CO., INC.
HALLANDALE, FLORIDA 33009

CONTENTS

Contents

Contents

CLOUD AND SILVER

CLOUD AND SILVER

ON BELLONA'S HEM

ALLIES TO THE END

(*December 1914*)

WE were sitting in a little restaurant in the Gay City—which is not a gay city any more, but a city of dejection, a city that knows there is a war going on and not so long since could hear the guns. There are, however, corners where, for the moment, contentment or, at any rate, an interlude of mirth, is possible, and this little restaurant is one of them. Well, we were sitting there waiting for coffee, the room (for it was late) now empty save for the table behind me, where two elderly French bourgeois and a middle-aged woman were seated, when suddenly the occupant of the chair which backed into mine and had been backing into it so often during the evening that I had punctuated my eating with comments on other people's clumsy bulkiness—suddenly, as I say, this occupant, turning completely round, forced his face against mine and, cigarette in hand, asked me for a light. I could see nothing but face—a waste of plump ruddy face set deep between vast shoulders, a face garnished with grey beard and moustache, and sparkling moist eyes behind highly magnifying spectacles. Very few teeth and no hair. But the countenance as a whole radiated benignancy and enthusiasm; and one thing, at any rate, was clear, and that was that none of my resentment as to the restlessness of the chair had been telepathed.

Would I do him the honour of giving him a light? he asked, the face so close to mine that we were practically touching. I reached out for a match. Oh no, he said, not at all; he desired the privilege of taking the light from my cigarette, because I was an Englishman and it was an honour to meet me, and—and—— "Vive l'Angleterre!" This was all very strange and disturbing to me; but we live in stirring times, and nothing ever will be the same again. So I gave him the light quite calmly, not forgetting to say, "Vive la France!" as I did so; whereupon he grasped my hand and thanked me fervently for the presence of the English army in his country, the credit for which I endeavoured fruitlessly to disclaim, and then all the members of each party stood up, bowed to each other severally and collectively, and resumed our own lives again.

But the incident had been so unexpected that I, at any rate, could not be quite normal just yet, for I could not understand why, out of four of us, all English, and one a member of the other sex, so magnetic to Frenchmen, I should have been selected either as the most typical or the most likely to be cordial—I who only a week or so ago was told reflectively by a student of men, gazing steadfastly upon me, that my destiny must be to be more amused by other people than to amuse them. Especially, too, as earlier in the evening there had been two of our soldiers—real men—in khaki in the room. Yet there it was: I, a dreary civilian, had been carefully selected as the truest representative of Angleterre and all its bravery and chivalry, even to the risk of dislocation of the perilously short neck of the speaker.

It was therefore my turn to behave, and I whispered to the waiter to fill three more glasses with his excellent Fine de la maison (not the least remarkable in Paris) and place them on the next table, with our compliments. This he did, and the explosion of courtesy and felicitations that followed was terrific. It flung us all to our feet, bowing and smiling. We clinked glasses, each of us clinking six others; we said "Vive la France!" and "Vive l'Angleterre." We tried to assume expressions consonant with the finest types of our respective nations. I felt everything that was noblest in the British character rushing to my cheeks; everything that was most gallant and spirited in the French temperament suffused the face of my new friend, until I saw nothing for him but instant apoplexy. Meanwhile he grasped my hand in his, which was very puffy and warm, and again thanked me personally for all that "ces braves Anglais" had done to save Paris and la belle France.

Down we all sat again, and I whispered to our party that perhaps this was enough and we had better creep away. But there was more in store. Before the bill could be made out—never a very swift matter at this house—I caught sight of a portent and knew the worst. I saw a waiter entering the room with a tray on which was a bottle of champagne and seven glasses. My heart sank, for if there is one thing I cannot do, it is to drink the sweet champagne so dear to the French bourgeois palate. And after the old fine, not before it! To the French mind these irregularities are nothing; but to me, to us. . . .

There however it was, and, in a moment, the genial enthusiast was again on his feet. Would we not join them, he asked, in drinking a glass of champagne to the good health and success of the Allies? Of course we would. Instantly we were all standing again, all clinking glasses again, all again crying "Vive la France!" "Vive l'Angleterre!" to which we added, "À bas les Boches!" all shaking hands and looking our best, exactly as before. But this time there was no following national segregation, but we sat down in three animated groups and talked as though a ban against social intercourse in operation for years had suddenly been lifted. The room buzzed. We were introduced one by one to

Madame, who not only was my friend's wife, but, he told us proudly, helped in his business, whatever that might be; and Madame, on closer inspection, turned out to be one of the capable but somewhat hard French women of her class, with a suggestion somewhere about the mouth that she had doubts as to whether the champagne had been quite a necessary expense—whether things had not gone well enough without it, and my contribution of fine were the fitting conclusion. Still, she made a brave show at cordiality. Then we were introduced to the other gentleman, Madame's cousin, who, we were told with pride, had a son at the Front; on hearing which, we shook hands with him again, and then gradually set about the task of disentanglement, and at last got into our coats and made our adieux.

When I had shaken his feather-bed hand for the last time my new friend gave me his card. It lies before me as I write, and I do not mean to part with it:

BAPTISTE GRIMAUD
DELEGUE CANTONAL
9A PLACE GAMBETTA
Pompes Funèbres

Well, if ever I come to die in Paris I know who shall bury me. I would not let any one else do it for the world. Warm hearts are not so common as all that!

MY FIRST BATTLE-FIELD

(December 1914)

THERE was a battle-field, I was told, with a ruined village near it, at Meaux, about thirty miles from Paris, and I decided to make every effort to see it. The preliminaries, they said, would be difficult, but only patience was needed—patience and one's papers all in order. It would be necessary to go to the War Bureau, beside the Invalides.

I went one afternoon to the War Bureau beside the Invalides. I rang the bell, and a smiling French soldier opened the door. Within were long passages and other smiling French soldiers in little knots guarding the approaches, all very bureaucratic. The head of the first knot referred me to the second knot; the head of the second referred me to a third. The head of this knot, which guarded the approach to the particular military mandarin whom I needed or thought I needed, smiled more than any of them, and, having heard my story, said that that was certainly the place to obtain leave. But it was unwise and even impossible to go by any other way than road, as the railway was needed for soldiers and munitions of war, and therefore I must bring my chauffeur with me, and his papers too would need to be in order.

My chauffeur? I possessed no such thing. Necessary then to provide myself with a chauffeur at once. Out I went in a fusillade of courtesies and sought a chauffeur. After countless rebuffs I hailed a taxi, driven by a vast grey hearthrug, and told him my difficulties, and he at once offered to drive me anywhere and made no bones about the distance whatever. So it was arranged that he should come for me on the morrow—say Tuesday, at a quarter to eleven, and we would then get through the preliminaries, lunch comfortably by noon and be off and away. So do hearthrugs talk with foreigners—light-heartedly and confident. But Mars disposes. For when we reached the Bureau at a minute after eleven the next morning the smiling janitor told us we were too late. Too late at eleven? Yes, the office in question was closed between eleven and two; we must return at two. "But the day will be over," I said; "the light will have gone. Another day wasted!"

Nothing on earth can crystallise and solidify so swiftly and implacably as the French official face. At these words his smile vanished in a second. He was not angry or threatening—merely granite. Those were the rules, and how could any one question them? At two, he repeated; and again I left the building, this time not bowing quite so effusively, but suppressing a thousand criticisms which might have been spoken were the French not our allies.

Three hours to kill in a city where everything was shut. No Louvre, no Carnavalet. However, the time went, chiefly over lunch, and at two we were there again, the hearthrug and I, and were shown into a waiting-room where far too many other persons had already assembled. To me this congestion seemed deplorable; but the hearthrug merely grinned. It was a new experience to him —and his metre was registering all the time. We waited, I suppose, forty minutes, and then came our turn, and we were led to a little room where sat a typical French officer at a table, white moustached and in uniform with blue and red about it. I bowed, he bowed, the hearthrug grovelled. I explained my need, and he replied instantly that I had come to the wrong place; the right place was the Conciergerie.

Another rebuff! In England I might have informed him that it was one of his own idiotic men who had told me otherwise, but of what use would that be in France? In France a thing is or is not, and there is no getting round it if it is not. French officials are portcullises, and they drop as suddenly and as effectively. Knowing this, so far from showing resentment or irritation, I bowed and made my thanks as though I had come for no other purpose than a dose of expensive frustration; and again we left the Bureau.

I re-entered the taxi, which, judging by the metre, I should shortly have completely paid for, and we hurtled away (for the hearthrug was a demon driver) to Paris's Scotland Yard. Here were more passages, more little rooms, more inflexible officials. I had bowed to half a dozen and explained my errand before at last the right one was reached, and him the hearthrug grovelled to again and called "Mon Colonel." He sat at a table in a little room, and beside him, all on the same side of the table, sat three civilians. On the wall behind was a map of France. What they did all day, I wondered, and how much they were paid for it; for we were the only clients, and the suggestion of the place was one of anecdotage and persiflage rather than toil. They acted with the utmost unanimity. First "Mon Colonel" scrutinised my passport, and then the others, in turn, scrutinised it. What did I want to go to Meaux for? I replied that my motive was pure curiosity. Did I know it was a very dull town? I wanted to see the battle-field. That would be triste. Yes, I knew, but I was interested. "Mon Colonel" shrugged and wrote on a piece of paper and passed the paper to the first civilian, who wrote something else and passed it on, and finally the last one getting it, discovered a mistake in the second civilian's writing, and the mistake had to be initialled by all four, each making great play with one of those hand blotters without which French official life would be a blank, and at last the precious document was handed to me, and I was really free to start. But it was now dark.

. . . . . .

The road from Meaux leaves the town by a hill, crosses a canal, and then mounts and winds, and mounts again, and dips and mounts, between fields of stubble, with circular straw-stacks as their only occupant. The first intimation of anything untoward, besides the want of life, was, on the distant hill, the spire of the little white village of Barcy, which surely had been damaged. As one drew nearer it was clear that not only had the spire been damaged, but that the houses had been damaged too. The place seemed empty and under a ban. Why from yet far away one village should look cursed and another prosperous, I cannot say; but this one suggested only calamity, and as one drew nearer its fate became more certain.

I stopped the car outside, at the remains of a burned shed, and walked along the desolate main street. All the windows were broken; the walls were indented in little holes or perforated by big ones. The roofs were in ruins. Here was the post office; it was now half demolished and boarded up. There was the inn; it was now empty and forlorn. Half the great clock face leant against a wall. Every one had fled—it was a "deserted village" with a vengeance: nothing left but a few fowls. Everything was damaged; but the church had suffered most. Half of the shingled spire was destroyed; most of the roof and the great bronze bell lay among the débris on the ground. It is as though the enemy's policy was to intimidate the simple folk through the failure of their supernatural stronghold. "If the church is so pregnable, then what chance have we?"—that is the question which it was perhaps hoped would be asked. Where, I wondered, were those villagers now, and what were the chances of the rebuilding of these old peaceful homes, so secure and placid only four months ago?

And then I walked to the battle-field a few hundred yards away, and only too distinguishable as such by the little cheap tricolours on the hastily-dug graves among the stubble and the ricks. Hitherto I had always associated such ricks with landscapes by Monet, and the sight of one had recalled the other; but henceforward when I see them I shall think of these poor pathetic graves sprinkled among them, at all kinds of odd angles to each other—for evidently the holes were dug parallel with the bodies beside them—with each a little wooden cross hastily tacked together, and on some the remnants of the soldier's coat or cap, or even boots, and on some the red, white, and blue. As far as one could distinguish, these little crosses broke the view; some against the sky-line, for it is hilly about here, others against the dark soil.

It was a day of lucid November sunshine. The sky was blue and the air mild. A heavy dew lay on the earth. Not a sound could be heard; not a leaf fluttered. No sign of life. We (for the hearthrug had left his car and joined me) we were alone, save for the stubble and the ricks and the wooden crosses and the little flags. How near the dead seemed! much nearer than in any cemetery.

Suddenly a distant booming sounded; then another and another. It was the guns at either Soissons or Rheims—the first thunder of battle I had ever heard.

Thus I too, non-combatant as *Anno-Domini* forces me to be, learned something of war—a very little, it is true, but enough to make a difference in reading the letters from the trenches or meeting a wounded soldier or a Belgian refugee. For I had gained a permanent background for their tragedies.

THE MARNE AFTER THE BATTLE

IN the destruction of the Marne villages there was much caprice. This one is destroyed: that unharmed. This one, such as Revigny, which is, however, bigger than a village, is carefully divided into two halves, one left as it was and one ruined. Vitry-le-François, a large market town on the great canal that eventually joins the Rhine, was only looted; Sermaize-les-Bains, an inland watering-place, was almost totally destroyed. At Heiltz-le-Maurupt, partly no doubt to show with what skill they could control their incendiarism, the Germans carefully isolated a Protestant chapel.

. . . . . .

Only one house, and that a large farm useful to the enemy, on the outskirts, remains at Vassincourt, a high-standing village where hard fighting occurred. Many were the killed, and the graves are so shallow that it is now far from sanitary. At the Café des Ruines, a mere shed which has sprung up, is pinned to the wall a piece of canvas: a relic of poor Pegoud's aeroplane sent to the proprietor by his soldier son. Another village almost wholly destroyed is Maurupt. And then, close by these, you find quiet villages that are as they were, except for a brooding anxiety. Here the Germans destroyed nothing, but merely took horses and food. In some cases, of course, the burning may have been disciplinary; in some cases the shelling was part of a genuine battle; but often enough the escape of one place and the destruction of another was due to mere differences of character in the enemy's commanding officers—this one being humane and that brutal, just as men may be in ordinary daily life.

. . . .

The churches have suffered very seriously, not without reason. Sometimes guns were mounted on them; often they were the scenes of bloody hand-to-hand conflict; while as coigns of observation their towers were naturally undesired by the invaders. There was therefore ground for their destruction. In many cases also they were as much hit by French as German shells, notably at Huiron, near Vitry-le-François, which stands, like so many Marne villages, on a high watershed. Huiron church is now just a husk. Over the door is a pretty sculptured saint, unharmed, as is so often the case in these church ruins. At Revigny the tower is smashed and the bell lies in fragments on the floor, but enough of the edifice remains for worship.

. . . .

Here and there one picks up stories of privation and fortitude, true enough but almost past belief. In one high-standing village, now ruined, for instance, was a man who, at the approach of the Germans, hurried to the forest of the Argonne with his dog. There he hid for three days with nothing to eat, watching the sky glow red with the flames of his own and other villages, and hearing the incessant guns. Then he ate his dog. Three days later he returned. He looks just like other men.

. . . . . .

At Maurupt is a small boy who, wandering in a wood just after the battle of the Marne, came upon a wounded German. What did he do? What should he have done? What would you or I have done? I cannot say. But the small boy returned swiftly to his home, obtained a chopper, and, saying not a word to any one, again sought the wood. . . . He is now a hero. If you go to Maurupt he will be pointed out to you.

. . . . . .

There are no young men in the villages; no men of middling age; only old men, women, girls, and children. The women do the work—drive the carts, control the harvesters, the mechanical reapers and binders (and the name of Pilter is probably better known than that of Poincaré in this district), milk, plough, sow. Were it not for the children, there would be no relief to the prevalent adult expression, which is sombre or resigned; and, indeed, acceptance of disaster may be said to be the new rural spirit, if the word spirit can be applied to such a negative state. September 6-12, 1914, left an ineradicable melancholy, so swift was the onrush, so terrible the rage, so irreparable and gratuitous the injury.

Is it to be wondered at that many of the old women confess to an upheaval of their faith? Why, they ask, should such calamity have come upon them? What had they done to deserve it? One old lady gives it out that she will trouble Joan of Arc, whose statue is in her village church, with prayers no more. "She has abandoned us," is her complaint.

. . . . . .

During the harvesting season regiments were sometimes billeted on villages for a month at a time, so that the soldiers might help in getting in the crops. For crops are needed not much less than the death of Germans. One of these soldiers was himself a farmer in the Midi. On his own distant farm were just two women, one very old, and his fields were lying idle with none to reap or carry. Meanwhile from dawn to dusk he harvested for a stranger.

. . . . . .

The ruins have a strangely foreign, un-French, appearance—due very largely to the chimney stacks which resisted the fire and for the most part still stand. They make the total effect one of a dead city of monoliths. Often no attempt has been made to remove any of the débris. Bedsteads twisted into odd shapes by the heat are very common objects. Bicycles similarly deformed are rarer, but one sees them, and almost always the isolated kitchen range, rusted and gaping but holding its own with a fine independence and determination, is visible. It seems to say that whatever else the Germans may have done they could not break the indomitable spirit of the French cuisine!

. . . .

Very little real rebuilding has yet been done—for who is to rebuild? Rebuilding needs strong men, and strong men are wanted more seriously elsewhere. Strong men are with their "Grand-père." But the French Engineers have put up wooden and tiled abris here and there, and the young men of the Society of Friends have been busy too; while hundreds of families still live in their cellars beneath a sloping roof. The huts built by the Friends are very simple: two or three rooms at most, with a roof of tiles or carton. The planks are of poplar, as they ought to be in the land of poplars: a tough fibrous wood, little used in England, but which in France is the favourite for sabots. Centuries ago, some one tells me, the Romans made shields of it. The Friends provide the labour and the cars; the French Government give the materials; but wood shortage is continual, since who is to cut it?

. . . .

The Society of Friends have been and are busy not only in hut-building but in all kinds of reconstitution: distributing seeds, chickens, rabbits, clothes, teaching the children, nursing, and so forth. For the Sinistrés, as the burned-out populace are called, naturally often lose all, and they need every kind of help in beginning again. How such stalwart young fellows in their grey uniforms first struck the simple and still half-dazed peasantry of the Marne, I do not know: but the subtleties of English sects and pacifism could not have been an open book. Watching several of the Friends at work on a shed, a curé put to me the very natural question, "Are all Englishmen carpenters?"

. . . . . .

The Friends' main field of labour in the Marne lies between Châlons-sur-Marne, Bar-le-duc, and Vitry-le-François. Sermaize-les-Bains, from which most of the operations have been directed, is in the midst of the triangle formed by these towns. Châlons is the great military centre, and there the Friends have a maternity hospital, and from Châlons their cars dash into Rheims to dare the shells and bring away patients. Later, I imagine the Friends will penetrate far into the Meuse and carry on their good work there.

. . . . . .

Vitry-le-François, named after François I, must be one of the neatest provincial towns in the world. Built by a monarch of orderly mind, though somewhat irregular habits (as one Diane de Poictiers could relate), it fulfils a rectangular plan. In the middle of it is a square; within that is a smaller square of lime trees, whose branches have been severely cut into cubes; and in the middle of that is a fountain. From this fountain radiate the four principal streets.

. . . . . .

The fountain itself, rather daringly in such close proximity to the real article, represents the Marne, that great and beautiful and very green and now poignantly historic river on which Vitry is situated. And the symbol of the Marne is, naturally enough in France, a bronze lady: a feat of imagery which, since the stream can be seen only a few yards away, should have the effect of turning the youth of the town either into poets or, by way of protest, realists. It suggests also that some limit of distance from the fact should be set upon symbolic sculpture. There, however, she stands, this bronze lady, not much more motionless than—especially on Sundays and in the evening—stand the multitude of anglers on her river's actual banks. For Vitry-le-François fishes with a unanimity and application such as I never saw before. Every one fishes: old women fish; young women; mothers with their children; girls; boys; elderly men; the barber with the strabismus who is so anxious to learn English; the tall man with one leg who manages his bicycle so cleverly: all fish. After five o'clock they are as sure to be by the river as the bronze lady is sure to be in the centre of the square. But, most of all, the soldiers fish. Vitry is packed with soldiers, and every one has a rod. When work is done they hold their rods over the river with a pacific content that for the moment reduces Guillaumism to a dream, a myth. But for that dread menace they would not be there in such numbers, it is true, yet how can one fear the worst so long as they angle, these warriors, with such calm and intensity?

. . . . . .

No one, so far as I know, ever catches anything; but what of that? It is notorious that fishing and catching fish can be totally opposed pursuits. Nothing ever discourages or depresses the Vitry enthusiasts. They fish on; they smoke on; they exchange jests and hopes. The barber, with his white jacket and his ragged beard, who for the most part has one eye on his float and the other on the street whence would come running the boy who lathers the customers, may now and then examine his hook with a gesture of surprise, but he is not really concerned to find no fish squirming there. Similarly, at intervals, every soldier withdraws his line to replenish his bait or move his float; but they too are not down-hearted. I say float, for it is wholly that kind of fishing. No flies, no reels even; nothing but a rod, a piece of string, a float, two split shots, a hook, and some quite superfluous lure. A few more imaginative minds add a landing-net. I have sometimes wondered what would happen if a fish with a sense of fun did once permit itself to be drawn from the river. Would they run as from a sea-serpent? I imagine them, en masse, soldiers and civilians, old and young, stampeding from the banks. "A fish! A fish!"

. . . . . .

Vitry has several inns, but only two that count, and one of these, the older and more stately looking, does not deserve to. It is ancient and mouldering, and nobody cares. You ring the bell, to no purpose. You ring again and again, and then discover that it is broken, has been broken for years. "La sonnette est cassée," you remark severely. "Oui," the patronne acquiesces, "elle ne marche pas." At this hotel nothing marches. In the stable are no horses; in the coach-house is one omnibus with three wheels and one with two. Progress not only has passed it by but has not even glanced at it.

. . . . . .

Vitry has also several cafés, one of which, by the canal towpath, where the weary horses plod, bravely calls itself the "Café de Navigation." As for the others, they are of the regular pattern —"de Commerce," "de Paris," and so forth. It also has many shops, for it is a centre of an agricultural district, and farmers and farmers' wives—chiefly farmers' wives nowadays—rely upon it for the necessities of life. And mention of the shops reminds me of an experience in Vitry which I shall ever cherish, for I too, finding myself one day in want of a necessity of life, entered the chief ironmonger's and laid my need before the assistant. A corkscrew? Assuredly. He had all kinds. He displayed first one and then another, remarking that the second was "plus sérieux." It was, of course, the more serious corkscrew that I bought. "Great sensible land of France," I said to myself, as I bore away this precious purchase, "where the words 'serious' and 'corkscrew' can be so naturally allied!" For the rest of my life corkscrews will fall into the two divisions—serious and the reverse.

. . . . . .

In a provincial paper, *Le Républicain,* published at Vitry, I find the following fine and tender letter written by a French soldier to a little girl who had sent him a gift. It has great and very French qualities, I think:

Du front, *le 16 mai 1915*

Ma chère petite fille

Je m'empresse de répondre à votre charmante lettre qui m'a procuré bien des émotions.

Par la même occasion je vous accuse réception du colis annoncé.

Votre petite lettre m'arrivant juste après le terrible assaut que nous venons de subir et au cours duquel nous avons eu la douleur de perdre notre capitaine, m'a encore plus impressionné.

Oui, chère petite fille, vous êtes encore bien jeune pour comprendre la vie, mais conservez cette lettre et dans quelques années lorsque vous serez plus réfléchie, vous pourrez comprendre combien il m'était doux de retrouver en vous les paroles et baisers de mes enfants que j'attends depuis plus de 10 mois.

Oui, c'est très bien de votre part cette généreuse idée suggérée par un professeur dévouée qui sait apprécier les craintes etles espérances d'un soldat sans nouvelles de sa famille et qui s'applique à le consoler.

Peut-être aurai-je un jour le bonheur de vous rencontrer, car les hasards de la vie sont si grands. Ce jour-là vous pourrez être assurée de trouver non pas un ingrat mais un second père.

Ma chère petite fille, mille fois merci ainsi qu'à votre professeur et ce sera avec plus d'ardeur encore et de bravoure que je lutterai pour la libération de notre chère France.

Espérons que ce beau jour n'est plus loin et recevez ma chère petite fille les meilleurs baisers d'un artilleur.

Signé: Jules Malaises

. . . . . .

Like all provincial French towns, Vitry has its share of clubs. I made a list of them for sheer pleasure in reading their friendly names. Here are some: Les Disciples de Progrès; Véloce Club Vitryat; Société des Combattants de 1870-71; Société des Sciences et des Arts; Les Fraternels anciens Sous-officiers; Jeunesse Républicaine Vitryate; and Société des Vétérans de Terre et de Mer. Can you not see them on Club nights? The animation of it all: the jokes, the laughter. I should like to peep in at the Combattants of 1870-71! white-moustached old fellows, some with only one arm or leg. And the veterans of the earth and the sea should be worth a visit.

. . . . . .

The Germans overflowed Vitry early in the war. The Mayor and Corporation fled, but the curé, a venerable and imposing white-haired figure, remained. I heard him tell the story in a sermon to the militaires, and it lost nothing in his rhetoric. The town would have been burnt but for the vast numbers of German wounded in it. A certain amount of looting was done, but not much. The Vitry people on the whole do not give the Huns such a bad character.

. . . .

It was at this special service in Vitry's great church that I felt the power of music as never before. Suddenly the first notes of a solo were heard in a tender, vibrant tenor. They broke on the ear without warning and came from I knew not where, but by moving my place—I was leaning against a pillar—I saw, high up, in the organ loft, the singer, a French soldier in khaki. He sang not only exquisitely but so movingly that it was almost pain, and yet such pain as one would not forgo. Hoping it might go on for ever, one trembled lest each note was the last. It was so beautiful that one feared to meet any other eye. . . . A little later he sang again. The first solo was a psalm, set to some wistful cadences; the second was a hymn, a long hymn enumerating the mercies of the Lord. Each verse began with the words "Souvenez-vous?" Did we remember? the singer asked us, in tones so gentle, so beseeching, and yet so rich that they touched chords that I did not know were hidden in me; and again the beauty of it was almost too much to bear. For the first time I realised that the voice is also an instrument. . . . Half the church was in tears. We heard later that the singer was a famous operatic star mobilisé.

. . . . . .

Sermaize, once an inland watering-place,—where the Friends have their head-quarters, housed oddly enough in an old casino, a disused petits-chevaux table serving as the director's desk,—is so ruined, and with such wantonness, that it would be an ideal spot in which (were it not that that building must be on conquered soil) to erect the pavilion where at the end of the war the representatives of the Powers might meet to confer as to terms of peace. With such surroundings our English tendency to forgive and forget could not but be interrupted. It would also, I think, be interesting and valuable if the demolished village of Vassincourt were retained exactly as it is and the new village erected at a little distance. Then for all time the methods of the Germans in a harmless agricultural district would be on record.

. . . . . .

One of the occupants of a Friends' hut who was imprisoned during the terrible week of the Marne battle had purchased some time before a coffre fort in whose impregnability she had so much confidence that she thought of the burning of her house comparatively undismayed. When, however, liberty came again and she hurried to the ruins to extract the safe and its contents, she found that it had played her false and everything inside it was incinerated. Among the things were various documents reduced to ash, and a jewel-case. The jewel-case she now displays to favoured visitors. It has nothing but its blackened treasures in it, but they are treasures none the less:—a ring with her father's hair, now dust; a ring with her grandmother's hair, also dust; a locket given her by her great lady (she had been a domestic servant); a brooch which had been her sister's; and so forth. The fire did not melt them; it merely turned them to dross. As she handles them tenderly one by one, the tears roll softly down her cheeks.

. . . . . .

All relics of the fighting have to be taken to the nearest mairies by order of the Prefect of the Marne; but it is a rule that is not too slavishly obeyed. The Mayor of Étrepy showed me many curiosities, including a vessel used by the Germans in gassing. After the enemy had passed and done their worst, great quantities of their inflammable gelatine disks were found here and flung into the neighbouring river Sault. They are square, the size of a quarter postage stamp, and as thick as sixpence. First, soldiers would pass down the streets flinging bombs through the windows, and then others would follow to throw in handfuls of these little fiendish squares to complete the conflagration. The Mayor led me to a field behind his new home and showed me the gun positions, and also a great black circle in the grass, covered with cinders. These, he said, were the remains of a funeral pyre of German bodies over which pitch was poured, there being no time to bury them. It is strange to hold in one's hand a piece of this slag—concentrated residuum of I know not how many of the foe.

. . . .

Every one is, of course, a souvenir-collector—in spite of the mairies. On most mantelpieces is a French 75 shell-case, and few men are without some pocket curiosity to display. The most interesting thing shown to me was a little fragment of red glass—picked up on the floor of Rheims Cathedral. One of the oddest German relics which I saw was a tiny book, all rain-stained and torn. It contained a series of rhymed protestations of affection and fidelity suitable to be written on post cards and sent back to Gretchen.

. . . .

In a wooden hut erected by the Friends lives an old woman to whose house came three huge and terrible Germans demanding food. They took all she had, chiefly potatoes; but even as they did so all three were killed. She now sits hour after hour at her door and sews; while under the potato patch in her little garden those three Germans lie.

. . . .

In another of the Friends' huts is an old woman who was imprisoned by the Germans for two or three days during the battle of the Marne, but, as she proudly records, they made no impression on her spirit. Not they! Not she! While under lock and key she noticed with anger a German soldier cleaning a coffee-cup with a lady's chemise of exquisite texture—probably snatched from the neighbouring château which they had carefully burned. Some time later the German, who could speak French, asked her if she would like a cup of coffee. "Have some coffee, grandmother?" were his words. "Yes—if the chemise is clean," she retorted. She tells this story with immense relish.

. . . .

During the summer of 1915 great supplies of crosses were prepared for the graves of the fallen, both French and German, in the department of the Marne. The German graves are marked by a railing and cross of silver birch, with the dead man's number affixed. The French graves have a more enduring painted wooden railing, a cross, and the tricolour. Often the poor fellow's képi is there too, and sometimes his coat and boots. When the grave is near habitations—and that means near a village, for there are no isolated houses—it often has flowers placed on it. The graves occur in the oddest places: in the midst of fields,—more than once I saw the tricolour just visible among the ripening corn,—beside the road, in front gardens and back. At Pargny, for example, there are several graves in a garden close to the railway, and just behind a neighbouring château three Germans lie, two named and one unidentified, but all commended to God's mercy. The château was closed, and one wonders if on the owner's return these graves will be removed.

. . . .

For the present, I believe, no French graves are to be disturbed; but in course of time the question of permitting relatives to remove bodies to consecrated ground may be considered. A certain amount of surreptitious removal was practised at first—very naturally, I think—but that was soon stopped. Of course private feelings have to be borne in mind, but where they are not strong I hope that the graves will remain scattered about as they now are. Probably a large number are certain to remain; and as it is, it is no rare experience to see a grave dating from the war of 1870—always an impressive sight.

. . . .

One thing is sure, and that is that the great composite graves must remain. Some of these, in the parts where an engagement was fierce, contain large numbers of bodies, even upwards of a hundred. There are some near Maurupt. For the most part they are distinct—the French lying together and the Germans lying together, and they are marked accordingly; but at one village whose name I forget, not far from Blesmes, is a grave in which a Frenchman who accounted for more than thirty of the foe is buried with them. The German officer who destroyed Sermaize by shell and fire is buried just outside the town, in a great sloping meadow, and with him are certain others. He had been wounded, but was writing triumphantly to his wife when the French dashed in and captured him. His wound proved fatal.

. . . .

In a mass of outbuildings which I visit—stables and lofts, dairy, wash-house and coach-house, now empty, but occupied by the Germans during the battle of the Marne for a night or so, and by many French regiments on their way to the Front since then—are a series of five little rooms, probably originally meant for grooms. Here at one time, for a rather longer period than usual, a group of French officers lived. Their names are on the walls, together with some of their portraits in silhouette (made by throwing the shadow of the profile with a candle, pencilling round the edges, and then blacking it all in), verses, mottoes, sentiments, such as "Vivent les femmes, le vin, et le tabac!" and a number of high-spirited drawings which, in the words of a curé who was with me, are distinctly "pas propres" and ought never to have met his virginal eyes. One of the poems enumerates the many gifts of a young officer of Zouaves, a very Admirable Crichton. His name is given. And when one reaches the end where the poet's signature is, behold the hero and his eulogist are one! Another is a savage attack by an assassin, in the manner of Aristide Bruant, on the judges of France. It would be interesting to know if the confessions in this strange doggerel were really autobiographical. There are enough to guillotine him.

. . . . . .

I was present in one village on the night that marching orders had come to the regiment which had been billeted there for some weeks. They were from the Midi, and spoke mostly the guttural French that one hears in Toulouse and Marseilles. The village street, the usual alternation of white cottages and farm-houses, was pitch dark save for the glimmering of light from a window here and there; and as it was full of wagons all ready for departure at daybreak, walking there was dangerous. Songs came from this room and that: ditties familiar to all, for all were sung in rich unison. Whenever a lull came one heard the low whispered tones of farewells in the darker corners. How many broken hearts these careless, homeless fighting-men leave behind them, who shall say? For they carry their facile affections from village to village as they steadily draw nearer and nearer to the Real Thing.

. . . .

In the hotel at Vitry was a French officer's fiancée, blonde and triste. He joined her at the table d'hôte, where they used to make plans, not with too much confidence: a little wistfully, and as though the gods might overhear. "Après la guerre," she would say, time and again, and he echoed it: "Après la guerre!" This phrase is the burden of conversation all over the country, from Calais to the Pyrenees, from Ushant to Marseilles —"Après la guerre!" Then what things will be done! For those who do not look too deeply or take long views, all that is joyful and perfect is summed up in these words, "Après la guerre!"

WAYSIDE NOTES

I Gratitude

I WAS sitting by my friend, the Captain, home on short leave, on the top of the motor-bus; where we were riding because of the fineness of the day and his desire to see more of that strange foreign city, London, rather than from necessity, for he is a landowner in the Shires and will have a good four-figure income to his name even after the Chancellor of the Exchequer has done his worst with it.

Well, we had not much more than established ourselves at Piccadilly Circus, going west, when an old lady on the seat in front of ours leaned back and spoke to my friend. She was one of those old ladies whose curves are all very soft. She had pretty grey hair, and gold-rimmed glasses, and the voice which, from its kind intonation, is usually called motherly, and no eyes whatever for the nice distinctions of military rank. Turning half round, she asked my friend what regiment he was in. He told her. And had he been wounded? No. But he had been in the trenches? Oh yes. And he was going back? Directly almost.

And here the conductor came up with "All fares, please." We felt for our money, but the old lady interposed. "Young man," she said to the Squire of ——, "I can't let you pay for yourself. I should like to pay for you. It's little enough one can do for our brave soldiers."

The poor Captain was for a second so embarrassed by her praise that he could say nothing; but there was a fine light in his face as he thanked her and watched her extract his penny as well as her own from the old-fashioned purse in her reticule.

"There," she said, as she handed the two coins to the conductor—"it would be a shame to let you pay that yourself."

These are the awkward moments. It was so comic and so beautiful; and I was glad when my friend, although we were far from our destination, stood up to descend.

On the pavement he spoke. "Another minute and I should have——"

"Laughed," I supplied.

"No," said the hero of a year's campaign, "cried."

II The Mistake

There is no need to specify the restaurant. It is famous for its English fare, and visions of its joints, pushed thoughtfully from table to table on little carriages by elderly white-robed carvers, are said to do more to sustain hope in the trenches than even the consolations of religion.

To one of the tables, provided with so many

chairs that secrets have ever been out of the question here, came two lieutenants, very obviously off duty for a brief season and rejoicing in their liberty; and he who was acting as host, and had long since settled all doubts as to what their meal was to consist of, flung out the order for roast beef almost before he was seated; flung it out too as though expecting as instant a response from the staff as he gets from his men, all unmindful that this restaurant has leisurely processes of its own, carefully acquired and perfected during many, many years.

Meanwhile the saddle of mutton was wheeled to my side and some unusually attractive slices were separated from it and laid before me.

I saw the lieutenants eyeing my plate with ill-concealed envy; but beef was in their minds. Beef had been in their minds for toilsome weeks, and they did not betray their friend. At least not wholly, but I fancy the host wavered.

"I wonder——" he began, and said no more, for the beef arrived on its little wagon, and their plates were soon covered with it.

It was not one of the most successful of the house's joints, and again I caught their eyes directed towards my saddle. Was it too late? their expression silently asked. Yes, it was. Besides, they had come there to eat beef. Nothing like beef!

The lieutenants attacked with vigour, but they still glanced muttonwards now and then, meditatively, between bites.

Then the host spoke. It was in an undertone, but I heard, because at this restaurant, as I have said, there are no secrets. "I wonder if we oughtn't to have had saddle?" he murmured.

"It looks jolly good," said the other.

They ate on.

"Do you think the beef is absolutely top-hole to-day?" the host asked.

"I've known it better," replied the other.

They ate on.

"I rather wish we'd had mutton," said the host. "After all—saddle, you know. It's not too common. Beef we can always get in some form or other—not like this, of course, but beef—whereas saddle, saddle's rare. I wish you'd reminded me of the saddles here."

"We'd settled on beef long ago," said the other, performing prodigies of valour with his knife and fork.

"I know; but it was foolish not to look at the bill of fare. I should have thought of it then."

They still ate heartily.

"No chance of getting here again for goodness knows how long," said the host.

The other dismally agreed.

"Could you manage a slice of saddle after this?" the host asked after a busy interval.

"Sorry I couldn't," replied the other, through a mouthful which a lion would not disdain.

"I don't believe I could either," said the host. "What a bore! I shall always regret not having had mutton."

"So shall I," said the other.

At this moment the empty seat next to me was filled, and to the inquiry of the head waiter, whose duty it is to ask these questions and then disappear for ever, the customer replied, "Saddle, of course. That's all one comes here for."

Both the lieutenants groaned audibly. Full though they were, their lunch, already ruined by me, was ruined again.

III Repentance

At the unusual sound of cheering in a London street—at so undemonstrative an hour as 9.15 a.m.—I turned and stopped. Down Charing Cross Road came three taxis, each containing many bags and many young men—certainly seven young men in each, packed high and low—and each containing two or more of that beautiful red, white and green flag which flutters so gaily and bravely over public buildings in Rome and Florence and Turin, in Venice, Verona and Milan, and on festa days (which seem to come seven times a week) in all the villages of the loveliest land on earth.

The young men waved and shouted, and shamefaced London, which has never yet cheered its own soldiers through the street, shouted back. For these were young Italians on their way to Italy, and there is something about a foreigner hastening home to fight for his country that would seem to be vastly more splendid than the sight of our own compatriots leaving home for the same purpose. So oddly are we English made.

Still, these young fellows were so jolly and eager, and, even in the moment of time permitted by their sudden apparition, it was so possible to envisage war's horrors in front of them, that no wonder there was this unwonted enthusiasm in the Charing Cross Road at 9.15 a.m. Besides, Italy had been a long time coming in . . .

A block brought the taxis to a standstill just by me, and I was conscious of something familiar about the youth in grey on the very summit of the first. He had perched himself on the fixed fore-part of the cab, and knelt there waving a straw hat in one hand and his country's flag in the other. And suddenly, although his face was all aglow and his mouth twisted by his clamour, I recognised him as a waiter at the—well, at a well-known restaurant, whose stupidity had given me from day to day much cause for irritation and to whom I had again and again been, I fear, exceedingly unpleasant. Less than a week before I had been more than usually sharp. And now I found myself trying to catch his eye and throw into my recognition of him not only admiration but even affection—a look that would convince him instantly that I wished every impatient word unsaid. But he was too excited to see anything in particular. His gaze was for the London that he had lived in and was now leaving, and for that London as a whole; and his thoughts were on his native land and the larger life before him. He had, very rightly, at the moment no eyes for one of those impatient, unreasonable and bad-tempered Englishmen known as customers.

In a few moments off they all went again, and with them went my thoughts—to their beautiful land of sunshine and lizards, of blue skies and lovely decay and absurd gesticulating men with hearts of gold. With them went my envy too, for it must be wonderful to be young and able to give up carrying plates and strike a blow for one's country.

Since then I have found myself saying to myself, I don't know how many times, "I wish he had seen me."

LAUGHTER IN THE TRENCHES

THE careless facetiousness of the British soldier in the fighting line of the present war is the wonder of the world. Where does he get this spirit? we ask. How comes it that, even there, jokes are so ready to his tongue? How can so much of his terrible business lend itself to jest? The complete answer would require a psychological memoir of great length, and no doubt we should in the course of it alight upon the fact that irony is allied to courage, or, at any rate, is one of the best protections against a too vivid perception of fact, and, collectively, an admirable means of concealing deeper feelings. But it is not the British soldier's use of humour as a sustaining influence in which I am at the moment interested, but his general day and night delight in it. This not only is new, but very curious.

For the best rapid idea of the persistent levity that I mean, one must go perhaps to the drawings of Captain Bruce Bairnsfather, collected in a book entitled *Fragments from France*. Here may be seen two score and more diverting pictures of Mr. Atkins at the Front informed by a sardonic laughing philosophy. The horrors of war are by no means lacking. Indeed, but for those horrors we should not have these jokes: the relation is intimate. No historian of the war who takes any account of the psychology of the New Army can afford to neglect Captain Bairnsfather's work. And it certainly reveals the value of irony as a prop in hard times. Without that buckler no trench fighter is fully armed.

What is the cause of this levity in this most cruel and terrible of campaigns? To a large extent fashion. Human nature, it is true, does not change, but human veneers change very often; and no doubt there is a fashion for facetiousness to-day that did not exist a few years ago. They had their jesters then, of course, but the joke was not essential; it was not yet crowned. To-day every one is funny, or would like to be funny. It is a kind of national duty. To-day the German trenches are given comic names, and bayonet charges towards them, which are to end in the bloodiest and most dreaded kind of warfare, are dashed into to such battle-cries as "Early doors, sixpence!"—a significant enough form of words, for it is largely through the music-hall and theatre that this prevailing and far from undesirable tendency to jest has grown and spread. Were I lecturing upon the two Georges—Mr. George Graves, with his grotesque epithet or simile for every incident of life; and Mr. George Robey, with his discoveries of the humour that lurks in seaminess—I should say that they are prime movers in this mode. Without them and what they stand for there would not exist half the raillery that now enlivens and heartens the army.

But there is still another reason for the levity of our men in this war; and that is the foe himself. Implacable and unscrupulous as the enemy has been, the German quâ German yet remains a comic figure to the mind of the English rank and file soldier, who is, one has to remember, very largely either the man in the street or the man in the village. To him the broad idea of the German, familiar, though not much considered, for years, is a quaint foreigner, often in too sharp competition with Englishmen, who shaves his head, usually wears spectacles, has an outlandish speech, is often too fat and always too alien; while it is notorious that he lives on sausages and that they are made of dachshunds. Probably the inseparable association of the sausage with Germany would alone have served to render the German a figure pour rire in the eyes of the unexamining, for, as has been often enough pointed out, it is sufficient to mention this article of diet to any English music-hall audience to have them in fits of laughter. Why, no one has ever wholly understood. For the comedian to say "kipper" is to partake of much of the same triumph, but not all. The sausage comes first, and the German, no matter what the rest of his activities may be, or how dreadful, is a sausage-eater or even sausage-worshipper.

Such, then, is the preconception, however erroneous, and it is so firmly fixed that not even the horrors of war can wholly exclude a certain amusement at the notion of this figure, indefinitely multiplied and clad in uniform, constituting the other side.

So much for those of our soldiers who had never met a German. There remain those that had, and here again was nothing to provoke anticipatory gloom, for the Germans visible and tangible to the man in the street and the man in the village are Germans who have shaved them, or fed them, or done them out of jobs; and none of them, despite their efficiency, were ridicule proof. There was something comic in the idea of an enemy consisting of this expatriated parasitical type of warrior. It made the campaign wear a farcical look. I do not suggest that there have not been very serious awakenings and realisations to the contrary, but the preconception gave the note and it has persisted. Moreover, when it is remembered that the British soldier is more ready to be amused than to be frightened, it will be seen that even the Germans themselves have contributed not a little to this risibility since the war began. That they devastated Belgium is true, but the deed carried its penalty with it in the name Hun, and to Mr. Atkins' whimsical mind such a word as that, and especially without the aspirate, is meat and drink. An enemy who, whatever his deadly purposefulness, can be characterised as 'uns is bound to attract banter. Then, again, there was the French soldier's word for him, also very sympathetic to the British sense of fun—Boche. The finer types of foe could never be called either 'un or Bosh; and when an 'ymn of 'ate is added there is no more to be said. In short, whatever the Germans have done, they have left a loophole, a joint in the armour, for the satirist to penetrate, and satire was never more general in England than now.

If one doubts that the alleged character and physical conformation of the enemy is in any way responsible for so much jestingness in our men, one has but to conjecture what would be the case were we fighting some one else. Did our men, for example, exhibit during the Crimean War anything approaching the sardonic mirthfulness of their present attitude? I can find no evidence that they did. And is it likely, were the Russians of to-day our foes instead of our friends, that our men would fight them laughing as they are so ready to laugh now? I think not, for the Russian is certainly not a figure of fun to the English mind. The mass of us know almost nothing about him, but what we do know, or think we know, is very serious.

Or against the French, should we be so light-hearted, so ready with hilarity? I think not. The Frenchman, once a target for English ridicule, has long ceased to be so. To this generation the term "Froggy" is hardly known. Moreover, the French, when it comes to warfare, have a tradition that carries a very impressive weight. They may have been beaten by the Germans in 1870, but Napoleon is still a gigantic idea, and atavistically we may yet be conscious of the Boney scares. Anyway, I hold that whatever preconception the man in the street and the man in the village may have fostered with regard to the French, there was no element of contempt in it. One reason for this I have given, and the other is that Frenchmen are rare in England, and when they are met they are not antipathetic enough for any very distinct preconception to have been formed, and certainly not one of disdain. It is the admirable nature of the French to wish to leave France as little as they can, and, once away, to wish quickly to be back again; and with such a nostalgia always present, they are concerned to take away no Englishman's livelihood. To a Frenchman there is no home but the country which it is foolishly customary to accuse of lacking a word for that sacred haven; whereas many Germans who bleat tearfully of their Fatherland are never happy until they substitute foreign soil for it.

THE SINKING OF THE U 29

By K 9

I AM one of the unhappiest of creatures, because I have been misunderstood. Nothing is worse than to mean well and do all you can, and still be misunderstood beyond any possibility of explanation. That is my tragedy just now, and it all comes of having four legs and no articulation, when the people who control things have only two and can express themselves.

"Sirius, how I ache! But let me tell you.

"I am a performing dog—nothing more and nothing less. I am associated with a man named—but perhaps I had better not give his name, as he might be still more cross with me, especially as he does not come too well out of this story. I am one—in fact, the principal one—of his troupe; and I have a number of quite remarkable tricks and the capacity to perform as many again if only my master would think it worth while to add to his list. But so long as there are so many music-halls where his present performance is always a novelty—and there are so many that he could be in a different one every week for the next ten years if he liked—why should he worry himself to do anything fresh? That is the argument he uses, not being a real artist and enthusiast, as I am, and as is one of my friends in the troupe too. She, however, does not come into this story.

"I don't know whether you know anything about music-halls, but it is my privilege to be in one and perhaps two every day, entertaining tired people, and the custom now is, if any striking news of the war arrives during the evening, for one of the performers to announce it. Naturally, since human beings like being prominent and popular as much as dogs do, a performer is very glad when it falls to him to make the announcement. Applause is very sweet to the ear, even if it is provoked merely by narrating the heroism of others, and it is not difficult for any one accustomed to hear it to associate himself with the action that has called it forth. I feel that I am very rambling in my remarks, but my point is that the privilege of telling the audience about a great deed just now is highly prized, and a performer who is foolish enough to miss the chance is stupid indeed.

"I must now tell you that my master is not the most sensible of men. It was clever of him to get into touch with so able an animal as myself and to treat me so sensibly as to induce me to stay with him and work for him; but his cleverness stops there. In private life he is really very silly, spending all his time in talking and drinking with other professionals, and boasting of the successes he has had, instead of learning new jokes and allowing me to do new tricks, as I should love to.

"Well, the other night, just as we were going on, some one brought the news of the sinking of the U 29. I heard it distinctly, but my master was so muzzy and preoccupied that, though he pulled himself together sufficiently to say 'Good business!' in reply, he did nothing else. He failed to realise what a chance it was for him to make a hit for himself.

"Look at the situation. On the one hand was the audience, longing to be cheered up by such a piece of news, and on the other a stupid performer too fresh from a neighbouring bar to appreciate his luck in having the opportunity of imparting it and bringing down the house. And not only that. For there was also myself—a keen patriotic British dog longing to tell the news, but unable to make all these blockheads understand, because with all their boasted human knowledge and brains they haven't yet learned to know what dogs are talking about. The result was—would you believe it?—my master began his ancient patter just as if nothing had happened. I tweaked his leg, but in vain. I snapped at him, I snarled at him, to bring him to his senses; but all in vain.

"Then I took the thing into my own paws. I ceased to pay him any attention. All I did was to stand at the footlights facing the house and shout out to the audience again and again, 'The U 29 has been sunk with all hands!'

" 'Come here, you devil,' said my master under his breath, 'and behave, or I'll give you the biggest thrashing you ever had.'

"But I didn't care. I remained by the footlights, screaming out, 'The U 29 has been sunk with all hands!'

" 'Mercy, how the dog barks!' a lady in a box exclaimed. Bark! I wasn't barking. I was disseminating the glad tidings.

" 'Silence, you brute!' my master cried, and brought down his little whip on my back.

"But I still kept on. 'They must know it, they must be told!' I said to myself, and I persisted with the news until at last the stage-manager rang down the curtain and our turn was called off. And a second later he was on the stage himself, apologising for my conduct and telling the audience about the U 29; and in their excitement they forgot all about their disappointment at not seeing me perform. Their applause was terrific.

" 'See what you missed by your folly,' I said to my master. But he paid no attention, he merely set about giving me the thrashing of my life.

"Sirius, how I ache!"

THE REAL HERO OF THE WAR

THERE is an impression about that among the candidates for the position of real hero of the war King Albert might have a chance; or even Lord Kitchener or General Joffre. But I have my doubts, after all that I have heard—and I love to hear it and to watch the different ways in which the tellers narrate it: some so frankly proud; some just as proud, but trying to conceal their pride. After all that I have heard I am bound to believe that for the real hero of the war we must look elsewhere.

Not much is printed of this young fellow's deeds; one gets them chiefly by word of mouth and very largely in club smoking-rooms. In railway carriages too, and at dinner-parties. These are the places where the champions most do congregate and hold forth. And from what they say he is a most gallant and worthy warrior. Versatile as well, for not only does he fight and bag his Boche, but he is wounded and imprisoned. Sometimes he rides a motor-cycle, sometimes he flies, sometimes he has charge of a gun, sometimes he is doing Red Cross work, and again he helps to bring up the supplies with the A.S.C. He has been everywhere. He was at Mons and he was at Cambrai. He marched into Ypres, and is rather angry when the Germans are blamed for shelling the Cloth Hall, because he tells you that there was a big French gun firmly established behind it, and only by shelling the building could the enemy hope to destroy that dangerous piece of ordnance. He was at Loos and Hooge. He saw something of the bombardment of Rheims, and he watched the monitors at work on the Belgian coast. His story of the landing at Suvla Bay is a marvel; and even more graphic is his description of the great evacuation.

And not only does he perform some of the best deeds and often get rewarded for them, but he is a good medium for news too. He hears things. He's somewhere about when General —— says something of the deepest significance to General ——. He knows men high up in the War Office. He refers lightly to K., and staff officers apparently tell him many of their secrets. He often has the latest Admiralty news too, and it was he who had the luck to be in the passage when Lord Fisher and another Sea Lord executed their historic waltz on the receipt of the news of Sturdee's coup. No one can give you so high a figure of the number of submarines we have bagged. Sometimes, I admit, his information must be taken with salt; but denials do not much abash him. He was prepared for them and can explain them.

His letters are interesting and cover a vast amount of ground. They are sometimes very well written, and in differing moods he abuses the enemy and pities them. He never grumbles but is sometimes preplexed by overwork in the trenches. He hates having to stand long in water, and has lost more comrades than he likes to think about. One day he was quite close to General Joffre, whom he regards as a sagacious leader, cautious and far-sighted; another day he was close to Sir Douglas Haig, and nothing could exceed the confidence which his appearance kindled in him. He is a little inconsistent now and then, and one day says he has more cigarettes than he can smoke, and the next bewails the steady shortage of tobacco. As to his heroic actions he is reticent; but we know that many of the finest deeds have been performed by him. He has saved lives and guns and has won the D.S.O. and even the V.C.

And what is his name? Well, I can't say what his name is, because it is not always the same; but I can tell you how he is always described by those who relate his adventures, his prowess, his news, his suspicions, and his fears. He is always referred to as "My son."

"My son," when all is said, is the real hero of the war.

VARIOUS ESSAYS

OF BAREHEADEDNESS

THE motto on the play-bill of a recent comedy stated that kings and queens have five fingers on each hand, take their meals regularly, and are, in short, the same as other people. But it is not true. No amount of such assurance will make kings the same as other people, because they are not. And the reason they are not the same is that they are different. I have just seen some of the difference.

I was leaving a London terminus, and, being with an invalid, I was travelling in a reserved compartment. Under the influence of well-directed silver bullets, porters had been skipping about in ecstasies of servility, and I was beginning to think myself almost one of the governing classes, when I observed two stationmaster persons in frock-coats and tall hats take their stand expectantly just by our carriage window; and one of our serfs came back importantly to inform us that a certain member of the royal house of England was travelling by the same train, and, in fact, would graciously occupy the very next compartment. Unhappily, however, this compartment was not on the engine side of ours, but on the other, so that although the presence of a traveller so august guaranteed a certain measure of safety, it could not absolutely eliminate risk for ourselves in the event of a collision, as it would, of course, have done had the salt of the earth been nearer the engine than we. Our assurance was limited to the knowledge that if a collision should occur its force would expend itself by the time our compartment was reached. We should be the ultimate victims. None the less it was comforting to be so near the Rose. Not the Rose itself, I must admit; nor even the Rose's consort. That much I may say, but beyond that I do not intend to divulge anything, merely remarking that though not a sovereign herself, there would be a different Kaiser in one country and a different queen in another had the lady who was about to take her seat in the next compartment possessed neither nephew nor daughter.

Well, suddenly a magnificent motor-car—so long and silent and luxurious that I marvelled at its occupants ever exchanging its warmth and security for a draughty terminus and a noisy railway train—drew up opposite our windows, and in a flash all head-gear was off—the two station-master persons' tall hats, the chauffeur's and the footman's caps, and the bowler of the tall deferential aristocratic gentleman who emerged from the car and helped the royal lady and her companion to alight. With the exception of the chauffeur and the footman, all, I may note, were partly bald. Then came a blossoming of courtesies on the part of the officials and acknowledgment of them by the visitors; nods and becks and wreathed smiles were exchanged; hands were even shaken; the royalty and her friend were ushered to their seats; the tall gentleman-in-waiting, who combined with the tactful aloofness of an undertaker the fluent ease of a diplomat and the authority of a commander, said a word or two to the railway representatives with a gay laugh, and disappeared into his own compartment, where doubtless he would kindle an expensive cigar; final salutations; and the train started, and heads once more were covered. Never had I occupied a private box so near the stage before.

And at our destination, which, as it chanced, was theirs too, we had all the comedy again, only here, in the provinces, there was a touch of gaucherie to help it. The Mayor was on the platform, hat in hand; near him were the chief constable and the stationmaster; and all were already bareheaded when the train drew up, and had perhaps been so for hours—the engine-driver being carefully instructed to operate his brakes to bring the royal compartment (and incidentally ours) abreast the welcome. All the members of the reception committee were again either bald or partly bald, so that I began to wonder if royalty's eyes ever alight upon a well-afforested head at all; and all received a gracious hand-shake. And again, having swiftly alighted from the train, here was the tall gentleman-in-waiting, hat in hand, a little rebuking to the Mayor by reason of his bowler, while his worship still clung to the steadily obsolescing topper. And so, in another storm of courtesies and acknowledgments, the royal lady drove off in the Mayor's carriage, and, a normal atmosphere having asserted itself, we plebeians were at liberty to descend.

But how can any dramatist pretend that kings and queens are the same as other people? And how, indeed, could they be the same, even if they wished, with all this ceremony of bare heads to set them back again in their place? For no one could stand it. In a very few days' time any man's character would, if all heads were bared directly he appeared, show signs of change. If one would remain ordinary and like unto the majority of one's kind, one must now and then be in the presence of a hat. To see nothing but scalps, whether or not covered with hair, indoors and out, cannot but make life artificial and rarefied. People in this position, with such an unvaried prospect, can never be like anybody else, no matter how regularly they take their meals or how normal their hands may be.

OF SILVER PAPER

OPENING a new box of cigarettes this morning, I came upon the usual piece of silver paper. But I did not as usual disregard it, but held it in my hand, examining it in a kind of wonder for some minutes, and asking myself why such beautiful stuff should be at the disposal of tobacconists in such profusion, how it was made, how it could be so cheap, and so forth. And I then shed some dozens of years from my shoulders by wrapping a penny in it and, by infinite smoothings with the back of a finger-nail, transmuting that coin into a lustrous half-crown—as I used to do when the world was young and silver paper a treasured rarity. And, having finished playing with it, I came back to the question, How is silver paper made? and from that to the question, How are most things made? and so to a state of stupor occasioned by the realisation of my abysmal ignorance. For I have no notion how silver paper is made, and I am sufficiently bold and sceptical to doubt too if the Swiss Family Robinson could have made it, to save their lives.

What would one first look for if one were told, out of a clear sky, to make some silver paper? Obviously not paper, for there is no paper about it; and obviously not silver, for if silver came into its preparation tobacconists and chocolate manufacturers could not throw it about as they do. Thus it is borne in upon me, and I recognise the verity with profound sadness, that, heir of the ages as I am, I am as ignorant of the making of silver paper as though I were a South Sea savage. Not only am I at a loss as to its preparation, but also as to what kind of people make it; where their factories are; what they call themselves. It may be a by-product of something else; it may be a business alone. Boys at Eton may be the sons of silver-paper makers or they may not. I don't know, nor do I know whether they would mention the source of their fathers' wealth or conceal it.

And I am equally ignorant as to the origin of thousands of other things which I fancy one ought to know. Looking round the room, my eyes alight on one thing after another. Colour printing, for example—how would one ab initio, set about that? An ordinary printing press I could see myself laboriously building up, with some rude success; but how do they take a Royal Academy picture, such as that on the wall above me, and translate it into mechanical reproduction? I have no notion beyond the vaguest. I know that photography comes in, and that three colours provide all the necessary tints and gradations; but how, I know not. And glass? What is the first step in the making of glass—that most mysterious of all substances: a great sheet of hard nothingness through which at this moment I watch a regiment of soldiers marching by? Could Robinson Crusoe have had glass? I feel convinced that he could not. Pens and ink, yes; and some substitute for paper (so long as it was not silver paper), yes; but never glass. Even such an ordinary matter as soap baffles me. I know that fat goes to its making, but I know also that, normally, fat rubbed on the hands makes them not clean but peculiarly beastly. How, then, does soap get its cleansing properties? I have no notion. And I am considered by those who meet me as not wholly an uninstructed man.

I look through my pockets. Money—yes, one could make some kind of an attempt at money, if one could get metal. A pencil?—yes, that is just black lead cut into a strip and enclosed in wood: easy. A knife?—not so simple, but obviously possible, because all castaways make things to cut with. Even, however, if I could not make these things, I know where they are made, and more or less how they are made. There are books to tell me this. What no book knows anything about is silver paper. Not even those friends of the ignorant, the Encyclopædists, help me. Their books lie before me, but all their million pages are silent as to silver paper; or if they do mention it, they carefully abstain from associating the information either with "paper" or "silver."

Did I, I ask myself, merely go to the wrong school, or are all schools equally taciturn about this kind of thing? There should be special classes for potential castaways. In fact, all education that does not fit scholars to be, one day, marooned, is defective: I would go as far as to say that. The height of mountains, the intricacies of algebra, the length of rivers, the dates of kings, matter nothing. But it does matter that one should know something about the ordinary daily things of life, their constituents and manufacture. Suppose the Government appointed me—as—after all the books I have written, with their show of information, it might easily do, at, of course, an insufficient wage—to be the companion of some gentle inquisitive barbarian visiting these shores—some new Prince Lee Boo—a nice kind of idiot I should look when he began to fire his questions at me! And silver paper is precisely the kind of glittering attractive stuff with which he would begin.

OF BEING SOMEBODY ELSE

WALKING along Oxford Street the other day, I was aware of a new kind of cheap photographer's into which people were pouring as though it were a cinema and Mr. Chaplin were on view. And, after examining the specimen photographs in the frame by the door, I joined them, not for the purpose of facing the camera, but to observe young men and women in the entertaining pastime of escaping from the fact, or, in other words, of assuming more agreeable identities than their own.

For the novel characteristic of this studio is that for the trifling sum of one shilling it provides its patrons with six post-card photographs of themselves in fancy dress; or, as a leaflet before me states, a shade too losely perhaps for Lindley Murray, but with perfect clarity, beneath a list of scores of costumes, "Every customer ordering six post cards for 1s. are entitled to use which one of these garments they think best, free of charge." What a privilege! The list is exhaustive. It begins with Cowboys, goes on to Cowgirls, Indian Chiefs, Indian Man, Policeman, Pierrots, Mexicans, Nuns, Whittington's Cat, Quaker Girls, Jockeys, Gent's Evening Suit, Gipsies, Highwaymen, Priests, John Bull, Cricketer,

Old Maid, Harem Skirt, Father Christmas, French Soldier, Aviator, Costers, Beefeaters, Buckingham suit, Nell Gwynne, Ladies' Evening Dress, Ladies' Tights, Boxer, King, Clown. The organisation is perfect. First the queue, then the ticket, then the choice of costume from the wardrobe upstairs, then the donning of it behind a screen, performed with infinite giggling when it is masculine and the wearer a girl, and then the taking of the photograph, which I can assure you is not allowed to occupy more than a few seconds. The only weak spot in the concern is the delay in developing and printing, for the client has to wait a day or so for the glorious results. Still, as a variation upon the drab routine of twentieth-century city life, not bad, is it?

Judging by specimen photographs of the happy masqueraders, the cowboy costume stands very high in favour and is the most popular male dress for young women. These are to be seen also in many varieties of man's attire, even to that of the police, looking for the most part smirkingly self-conscious but wholly satisfied. That no one would ever be taken in as to their sex matters nothing. A wooden horse of high mettle, obviously by a sire and dam with classic sawdust in their veins, lends verisimilitude to the cowboy illusion, and it is amusing to see this very recognisable noble animal turning up again and again in the pictures, always under perfect control. Some of the new Army doctors, who by the regulations are forced to wear spurs but have never spurred anything in their lives, might, by the way, like to know of this placid charger. They are certain to wish to distribute a few photographs of themselves.

I have made only a selection from the costumes supplied. I might have added many more, such as naval officers and Red Cross nurses, both of which, I am told, are in great demand. I might, too, have mentioned the one that, after the "Buckingham suit" (which is perhaps merely a euphemism for Court dress), is most perplexing to me. This is described curtly as "draper." Who on earth wants to spend a shilling to be photographed as a draper? And what is a draper's costume? I have seen thousands of drapers, but they did not differ from haberdashers, tailors, chemists, or hotel clerks. Dan Leno's shopwalker is probably the type selected—poor Dan having also confused the two functions; for a shopwalker only walks the shop, whereas the deathless figure invented by that ever-to-be-mourned comedian acted as a salesman too.

That the studio is a success was inevitable, and I expect a great crop of imitations. For it is based on a sound knowledge of human nature. Its originators know life. Every one who has ever been a child remembers the excitement of dressing up. No game without dressing up in it could compare with one in which a father's tall hat, a mother's best dress, and a hairy hearth-rug were introduced; and very few of us ever cease wholly to be children. As the poet says, "we are but children of a larger growth." Throughout life, for most of us, to be somebody else is the thing. Well, at this studio young people who are no longer children play at being children once more. After working all day as clerks, or shopmen, or typists, or domestic servants, how delightful to come here and evade destiny by masquerading as highwaymen, bush-rangers, Queens of the Carnival, Dreadnought commanders, and George the Fifth courtiers! Better still, how tonic to the self-esteem to be taken in the act of complete mastery of a spirited horse! And what pictures to send away! What gallant portraiture for the provinces!

And—if we only knew—what an invigoration of ordinary life for a while! I like to think that the effect upon a little lodging-house drudge of having been a Queen of the Carnival long enough for the evidence of the camera (which cannot lie) to be secured, cannot wear off at once. Surely she carries her head a shade higher in consequence, and bears the censure of her mistress with increased fortitude? I hope so: I believe so. And I can imagine a general toning-up of self-esteem in many a shop-bound youth in the knowledge, abundantly furnished by these postcards, that were he really the rightful possessor of a naval uniform he would not disgrace it, but pursue the *Schmutzigehund,* or whatever German cruiser came his way, as resolutely and effectively as Sir David Beatty himself; and this being so, in spite of fate's embargo, he does not do his less illustrious work any the worse. And many a seamstress might with more composure view her inability to be smoothing the pillow and winning the heart and hand of a wounded officer if her eyes could now and then be refreshed by furtive peeps at herself in a Red Cross costume, and see how well she would look as a nurse (her true vocation) if only the gods were kinder.

The strength of this studio is that in it the gods can be made kinder—momentarily.

OF PERSONS THAT WE ENVY

THE last of the Commandments (which a little American boy broke so easily and so often that he thought he might as well make a clean job of it and go on to break the Eighth also), the Tenth Commandment, mercifully omits the only thing about any of my neighbours that I have ever coveted—their characteristics—and therefore I assume that such covetousness is innocent. Certainly I can hear it declaimed by even the most minatory of clerics and turn no hair. To begin with, one's neighbours are usually so eminently persons to be avoided that the very idea of covetousness in connexion with them is grotesque. But reading a wider meaning into the word "neighbour" than it now has, there are certain people that one knows who possess some little personal gift or charm which one would not be unwilling to add to one's own repertory. If this is coveting, then most of us are guilty; but I have the conviction that coveting must have meant more than merely desiring, must in Sinaitic times have overrun into theft, to figure in the Decalogue at all. For coveting in the abstract is almost as natural as breathing, and indeed it forms a basic part of at any rate one of the qualities which we unite in praising—ambition.

Cloud and Silver

These thoughts were suggested to me last evening by overhearing the sudden heartfelt exclamation of a young woman, a total stranger, in an hotel chair near me, in one of those uncomfortable focuses of self-consciousness called a lounge. "My word, how I envy her!" she said, as another young woman went by, on her way from the table d'hôte; and straightway I fell to wondering if there was any one I too envied and what envy really meant.

An essayist recording the heroic renunciation of a sailor on the *Formidable,* who, himself an orphan, relinquished cheerfully his right to a seat in one of the boats to a man who had parents, and releasing his hold of the gunwale was lost in the angry winter sea, expressed a wish that he might in similar circumstances behave as well: a feeling which, with whatever misgivings, we must all share. But that is admiration, not envy. No one wants to be a drowned sailor, however glorious his end. No one envies him. We envy the living, and, I suspect, the older we grow, the fewer of the living do we subject to that operation. "How I wish I was So-and-so!" is the plaint of the young. The middle-aged know that the only thing in the world worth being is oneself, even with all oneself's limitations. But even the middle-aged can now and then wish for a modified transference of personality—for the grafting, upon their own otherwise unaltered stock, of a merit borrowed from this idol and that. "I wish I had So-and-so's easy manners!" we say. "I wish I could tell a story like Blank!" "I wish I could sing as Dash does!" "I wish I had Asterisk's memory for faces!" As a matter of fact we should not value any of these illicit acquisitions if we had them, since the whole structure of our personality would be disarranged and trouble would ensue; but light-heartedly we may express the wish. Well for us that no fairy is listening! Well for us that our heads, when we speak in this idle way, bear no magic caps!

Whom do you most envy? would be a good question to put to our friends. Putting the question to myself, I find that the one creature in the world whom at this moment I most envy—that is to say, who has eminently and glitteringly the characteristic which I most covet—is the lady of whom I was hearing recently, who on the evening of a dinner-party sought her room to dress, and did not re-emerge. Time passed, the guests arrived, every one was present but the hostess. People began to grow nervous; the mauvais quart d'heure took on qualities of turpitude beyond bearing. At last the missing hostess was sought for by her daughter, and found comfortably asleep between the sheets. Her forgetful mind, oblivious of the social engagement, but conscious of all the suggestion and routine of retirement, had sent her peacefully to bed. Now, there is a person whom I envy with all my heart, for I have never been able to do an absent-minded thing in my life, and I long for the experience. Existence would become simple if only I had a reputation for such vagaries. As it is, I am the one mechanical, punctilious person in my circle. I am the one who is never permitted not to answer a letter, forget an appointment, or let even the most casual undertaking be neglected. But with that lady's sublime gift of domestic aphasia I could really have a holiday now and then.

OF GOOD ALE

TWO things there are which, however rosily one may view the present, are never as good as they used to be. One is acting, and the other is ale. There are no actors, and (more particularly) no actresses, to compare with those of our youth; there is no ale such as we used to drink before we knew that we had to die. And we cling to both convictions the more tenaciously, possibly, because the excellence of both is now only hearsay. Our darling actresses (God bless them!) have retired, or are no more; the ale has long been drunken.

In particular is it true of ale that it is not so good as it used to be. That ale to-day is not what it was is notorious, for too many Chancellors of the Exchequer have been at it; and specific gravity is the modern brewer's fetish; and a thousand devices for superseding his intimate personal attention and even solicitude have come into action. But the evidence of a pleasant book which lies open beside me proves that as far back as the year 1750 ale had fallen far below its true level, the sole cause of this treatise being the decadence that had come upon John Barleycorn.

The book, the title of which is *The London and County Brewer,* 7th edition, 1758, is very English, very simple and enthusiastic, and wholly intent upon reformation. The author's name is withheld, but he is described as "a Person formerly concerned in a Publick Brewhouse in London, but for Twenty Years past has resided in the Country," and, to quote his own words from the preface: "By the Time the following Treatise is read over, and thoroughly considered, I doubt not, but an ordinary Capacity will be in some degree a better Judge of good and bad Malt-Liquors as a Drinker." This antithesis of an ordinary capacity and a drinker is pretty. He continues: "And therefore I am in great Hopes, these my Efforts will be one principal Cause of the reforming our Malt-Liquors in most Places; and that more private Families, than ever, will come into the delightful and profitable Practice of Brewing their own Drinks." Alas for that ideal! There can be but few private brewhouses left. Beer is under a cloud; our very monarchs drink barley-water.

Of all the many varieties of ale commended in this genial work, the author's favourite seems to be Devonshire White Ale. It was invented at the end of the seventeenth century at or near Plymouth, and the author's "eager Pen" (as he describes it) gives it such a character as we now associate not with alcohol but with patent medicines. "Those who are not too far gone in consumption" find it beneficial; it cures colic and gravel; and it is "the best Liquor in the World for a Wet Nurse to drink."

The modern brewer has given up the recommendation of his wares as the handmaids of

Æsculapius. But of old beer was much extolled in this way. In *The Unlettered Muse,* a rare volume of homely verse by John Hollamby, miller, of Hailsham, in Sussex, published in 1827, I find the following admirable Bacchanalian song in praise of the beer brewed by Thomas Gooche of Norfolk, who was brewing at Hailsham at that time. Here is the song:

GOOCHE'S STRONG BEER

"Fancy it Burgundy, only fancy it, and 'tis worth ten shillings a quart."

O, Gooche's beer your heart will cheer,
  And put you in condition;
The man that will but drink his fill
  Has need of no physician.

'Twill fill your veins, and warm your brains,
  And drive out melancholy;
Your nerves 'twill brace, and paint your face,
  And make you fat and jolly.

The foreigners they praise their wines
  ('Tis only to deceive us):
Would they come here and taste this beer,
  I'm sure they'd never leave us.

The meagre French their thirst would quench,
  And find much good 'twould do them;
Keep them a year on Gooche's beer,
  Their country would not know them.

All you that have not tasted it
  I'd have you set about it;
No man with pence and common-sense
  Would ever be without it.

"The meagre French" is good. It takes a Hailsham miller with a turn for verse to apply such an adjective to that nation. Had he travelled, or even read, he would have known better—and worse. For truth nearly always cuts into the picturesque, and injustice, which is the salt of international lampoons, dies in its presence. But what is there in the air of Sussex that so inspires that county's poets to the praises of ale? Mr. Belloc must turn aside from strategy for a moment to answer this.

When it comes to fancy beverages my own taste inclines to Cock-Ale. Of this exotic cordial I never heard before; and I am never likely to taste it. But here is the recipe, for the curious: "Take a Cock of half a Year old, kill him and truss him well, and put into a Cask twelve Gallons of Ale, to which add four Pounds of Raisins of the Sun well pick'd, ston'd, wash'd, and dry'd; Dates sliced Half a Pound; Nutmegs and Mace two Ounces. Infuse the Dates and Spices in a Quart of Canary twenty-four Hours, then boil the Cock in a manner to a Jelly, till a Gallon of Water is reduced to two Quarts; then press the Body of him extremely well, and put the Liquor into the Cask where the Ale is, with the Spices and Fruit, adding a few blades of Mace; then put to it Half a Pint of new Ale Yeast, and let it work well for a Day, and, in two Days, you may broach it for Use; or, in hot Weather, the second Day; and if it proves too strong, you may add more plain Ale to palliate this restorative Drink, which contributes much to the Invigorating of Nature." That sounds like the real thing. Will no one invite me to a dish of Cock-Ale?

Alas, the efforts of the gallant author of this book were not destined to be long successful. That they were operative for a score of years we know, for see what brave John Nyren said, when, in old age, he was speaking of the becoming revels of his youth on Broad Halfpenny Down during the great cricket matches in the seventeen-seventies. "The ale, too!" he exclaimed, in a famous lyrical passage, "not the modern horror under the same name, that drives as many men melancholy mad as the hypocrites do; not the beastliness of these days that will make a fellow's inside like a shaking bog, and as rotten; but barleycorn, such as would put the souls of three butchers into one weaver. Ale that would flare like turpentine—genuine Boniface! This immortal viand (for it was more than liquor) was vended at twopence per pint. The immeasureable villainy of our vintners would, with their march of intellect (if ever they could get such a brewing), drive a pint of it out into a gallon." That, as I say, was in the seventeen-seventies, and I like to attribute the excellence of the Nappy of that day to the powerful although alas! fleeting influence of *The London and County Brewer*.

OF THE BEST STORIES

I WAS reading the other day that that most amusing of clerks in holy orders, who writes Irish farcical stories over the pseudonym: "G. A. Birmingham," but is known to the angels as Canon Hannay, has given it as his opinion that the best funny thing ever said is Charles Lamb's reply to the doctor who recommended him to take a walk on an empty stomach. "Whose?" inquired Lamb. That certainly is among the best of the comic remarks of the world; but why does Canon Hannay put it down to Lamb? All my life I have been associating it with another humorous clerk in holy orders and also a canon, the Rev. Sydney Smith, and it is to be found in every collection of his good sayings. Canon Hannay, who is normally so eager to give the Church even more than her due,—for did he not create out of "J. J." the curate a super-magazine-hero, blending Sherlock Holmes, Captain Kettle, and Terence Mulvaney in one?—Canon Hannay, one would think, would have naturally allotted Sydney Smith everything. Moreover, the joke is more in Sydney Smith's way than in Lamb's; not because Lamb was not expert at that peculiar variety of nonsense, but because Lamb had a passion for walking, and rarely, I should say, suffered from any malady needing this particular remedy; whereas the witty canon was a diner-out, addicted to gout and other table afflictions, and a walk on an empty stomach would probably have done him a world of good.

And now I lay aside my pen for a few moments in order to wonder what my own favourite story is, and have the usual difficulty in remembering any stories at all. Searching my memory, I find that Lamb comes up first, which is not unnatural, for in the stories which most appeal to me there must be irresponsibility rather than malice. Malice is easier, for one thing, and the laughter it causes is of an inferior quality. That touch of gay nonsense which Lamb had, and Sydney Smith had, is worth (to me) all the brilliant bitternesses. This time, too, it is authentic Lamb, and not Brummagem. My momentary choice is Lamb's reply to the reproach of his India House superior, "You always come late to the office." "Yes, but see how early I leave!" That could not easily be beaten.

Lamb, however, did not consider that his best thing. We have it on evidence that he thought his not too kindly remark to his friend Hume on the size of Hume's family his best joke; but I, for one, do not agree with him. Hume, it seems, was the father of a numerous brood, and he happened once to be so ill-advised as to mention his paternal achievement, apparently with pride, in Lamb's presence. "One fool," quoted Lamb, "makes many." Personally, I don't much esteem this story, not only because it is a score off a simple creature, and a rather too facile one at that, but also because it comes into the category of those sayings which the joker must himself have reported, or which the recipient of the witticism could not well report except resentfully. We can imagine the auditor of the priceless reply, "But see how early I leave," after recovering from the stunned condition into which its tremendous irrelevance and foolishness knocked him, hurrying away in perplexity to report it in all its incredibleness to fellow-officials: "What on earth do you think that that mad creature Lamb has just said to me?" and so on. But one does not see Hume hastening round to spread that family joke. Lamb, or another, must himself have done it.

Similarly, when the Austrian journalist Saphir, who said so many witty things, met an enemy in a narrow passage, and on the enemy remarking, "I'll not make way to let a fool pass," pressed himself against the wall, saying, "But I will," it must have been Saphir who took the glad tidings round Vienna. A man, said Lamb (and proved it, too), may laugh at his own joke; but I think we always rather prefer that it should first get into currency by the other fellow's agency.

And yet, if that rule were strictly followed we should lose too many good things, for your true humourist scatters his jewels indiscriminately and does not reserve them for the fitting ear.

Sir Walter Raleigh (I mean not the explorer but the longest knight) has pointed out that the reason why we have comparatively so few records of Lamb's jokes is that he made them to simple people, who either did not understand how good they were, or were not in the way of quoting them. As a friend of mine, who does something in a waggish line himself, remarked sadly to me the other day: "I am always saying the right thing to the wrong people. Some one asked me the other day if I had known William Sharp. 'No,' I said, 'but I once met Wilfrid Blunt,' and instead of laughing my friend began to talk seriously of the *Sonnets of Proteus.* I have no luck." The fact is that what all wits need is a Boswell. Without a Boswell it is necessary, if they are to be reported, that they must either themselves publish their good things or keep on repeating them until the right listener hears and notes them. Had there been a Boswell for Lamb. . . . But Lamb could not have endured one.

Having reached that point in this discursion, I sallied forth to the haunts of men to collect other opinions as to the best story. One of them at once gave Sydney Smith's reply to the little girl who was stroking the tortoise's shell, "because the tortoise liked it." "As well stroke the dome of St. Paul's," said Sydney, "to please the Dean and Chapter." A second choice shakes me seriously in my own selection, for it ranks high indeed among the great anecdotes. Sam Lewis, the money-lender, was, at Monte Carlo, a regular habitué of the Casino. One day he bade every one farewell. "I shan't see you for a fortnight or so," he said; "I'm off to Rome." "Rome?" they inquired in astonishment. "Yes. I'm told it's wonderful." Two or three nights later he was back in his seat at the gambling table. "But what about Rome?" his friends asked. "You can 'ave Rome," said Sam.

A third offered an historic dialogue from the Lobby. It seemed that an M.P., whom we will call X., somewhat elevated by alcohol, insulted another M.P., whom we will call Y., as he passed through that sacred apartment, by calling him "a —— fool." Y., stopping, said severely and pityingly, "X., you're drunk. I shall take no notice of what you say." "I know I'm drunk," replied X., "but *I* shall be all right to-morrow. You're *always* a —— fool."

Since writing the last paragraph I have asked two more friends for their favourite stories. One of them at once gave me Whistler's comment on reading in the *Reminiscences* of W. P. Frith, R.A., painter of "The Derby Day," that as a youth it was a toss-up which he became: an auctioneer or an artist. "He must have tossed up," said Whistler. The other choice was American and more cynical. A man's wife had died, and on the morning of the funeral the man was found sitting on his doorstep whistling gaily as he whittled a stick. One of the mourners remonstrated. It was most unseemly, he pointed out, that the widower should be thus employed on the day on which they were bearing to her last resting-place the remains of a woman so beautiful in person and in character—

a faithful wife, a fond mother, an inspiration and model to the neighbourhood. "Don't you realise that she was all this?" the scandalised guest inquired. "Oh yes," said the husband, "but—I didn't like her."

And now, having set down all these examples, I remember what probably is the best good thing of all. For, as every one knows, there is some malign fate which has provided that one's memory shall always be a little late when the best stories are being swapped. But better late than never. Dumas père, it may not be generally known, had African blood. He also was the father (like the great Sheridan) of a witty son. Said Dumas fils one day, of his sublime sire: "My father is so vain and ostentatious that he is capable of riding behind his own carriage to persuade people that he keeps a black servant." Having recalled that of Dumas fils, here is the best story that I know of Dumas père. Perhaps it is as good a story as has ever been told of any egoist. Coming away from dinner at a house noted for its dulness, he was asked by some one if he had not been dreadfully bored. "I should have been," he replied, "if *I* hadn't been there."

But of course these are not the best stories. Another day's memory would yield far better ones.

OF MONOCLES

"NO man"—the wife of one of our most famous novelists was speaking—"can wear a single eyeglass and not be in some respects a fool." I considered for a while, and then told her that I thought she was too sweeping; but she would not give way. In so far as that the presence of one eye only with a window to it imparts a ludicrous appearance, which can easily be consonant with folly, she is right; but there are exceptions. Take the case of Mr. Dennis Eadie as an instance; for right through *The Man Who Stayed at Home* he suggested folly and inoperativeness, only that his final triumph of cleverness might be the more complete. The lady has, however, all the tradition of the stage on her side, for the first instinct of any actor cast for the part of a Society ass is to provide himself with a monocle.

The facial distortions and contortions necessary for the adjustment of the monocle have indeed made the fortune of more than one piece; and the implement itself has done much for others. Lord Dundreary I never saw, but I take it that it was he, or rather the great Sothern, who fixed the place of the eyeglass in dramatic history, and thus in the mind of the public. Mr. G. P. Huntley I see as often as I can manage, and he it is who is chiefly instrumental in keeping the eyeglass convention alive to-day. Without it he would be only half as delightful as he always is. None the less, one or two of the astutest men that I know wear these things, and the late Mr. Joseph Chamberlain, whatever there may have been against him, was not often charged with foolishness. But Mr. Chamberlain did as much to dignify the monocle as other men have done to make it absurd.

I suppose that the date of the first appearance of the monocle is known; but my encyclopædia does not condescend to such trifles. Spectacles it knows all about. Spectacles, it seems, were invented either by Alessandro di Spina, a monk who died at Pisa in 1313, or Salvino degli Amati, who died in Florence four years later. Somehow I had thought of the Chinese, always so anticipatory of civilisation, as owning the credit for this invention; but it is pleasant to be able to place it with our Allies. Having stated the fact, however, the encyclopædist, in the usual style of such imparters of information, goes on to cloud the issue and bemuse the student by saying that an Arab writer of the eleventh century mentions them. So there you are! But nothing of the monocle.

It is, I suppose, the want of balance, the asymmetry of the single eyeglass, that has largely brought it under suspicion; and also the circumstance that peculiarities of sight are not much understood by the people, with whom ridicule starts. If working-men ever wore single eyeglasses we should hear little on the subject; but so long as—as at present—a navvy in a monocle would be a more rare and amazing phenomenon than a submarine in Pall Mall, so long will the unfortunate possessor of one good eye and one defective one be a figure of fun to the masses. A man may have one crutch, or one arm in a sling, and no one laughs; but for one eye only to be defective and therefore glazed, while the other is sound and therefore nude, is a perpetual and gigantic joke.

Much of the ridicule caused by monocles is based also on scepticism. I believe that if a plébiscite could be taken it would be found that the vast majority of people are convinced that single eyeglasses are an affectation. No doubt that is so in many cases. No doubt many a youth wishing, as one might euphemistically put it, to graduate at the University of Barcelona, has paid as much attention to acquiring the art of wearing an eyeglass as to the choice of socks or the arrangement of his chevelure. Many an older man coming whole-heartedly into the classification of the novelist's wife quoted above has also, though sound of vision, deliberately selected the monocle as a symbol of doggishness or aristocracy. Such impostors, harmless enough, but far from admirable, civilisation can always produce.

Yet a residuum of genuine monocle-wearers remains, certain representatives of which I am happy to number among my friends. Among these is one, not unconnected with literature, who is almost blind without his auxiliary. To him, however, the thing is a matter of jest, and in moments of levity he will transfer it to his forehead, cheek, or even the tip of his nose. He carries no cord, but in his pockets is a reserve supply of glasses, so that if one falls and breaks (as always happens) another can instantly supply its place. And once I knew a woman who wore a monocle; and a frightening figure she was. That it was necessary was proved by the size of the eye seen through it, which was magnified inordinately. Even without this appurtenance she would have been uncannily masculine, and, like all masculine women, a horror; but with it she terrified my youthful life. Whatever may be said for the monocle, one thing is certain, and that is that it is not woman's wear.

OF SLANG—ENGLISH AND AMERICAN

I WAS hearing the other day of a famous girls' school where slang is forbidden. A certain caprice, however, marks the embargo, for "topping" is permitted although "ripping" is on the black list. Personally I wish that at all schools slang of every kind was strictly discouraged, for it leads to the avoidance of any effort to be precise in speech; it tends to slovenliness. At lunch recently, for example, I sat next a young woman, a mother, who was telling me of her experiences in Venice. I asked her what she thought of that city of wonder. "Topping," she replied, and then added, thoughtfully, "Topping." Now I did not expect her to deliver a lecture on the charms of Venice and to give me an analysis of her many emotions on first seeing them, but I confess that I was looking for something a little more descriptive than the word she selected. There is no doubt that Venice is topping, but then so is the cooking at the Focus, and so is the new revue at the Futility, and so is the dress your cousin wore at her coming-out dance, and so is Miss Hieratica Bond's new novel.

The trouble with English slang is that it is seldom descriptive, seldom paints pictures, seldom contains an idea. Probably no word signifying excellence has been so much used as "ripping," but how does it come to mean that? "Topping" one can derive: it savours of the top, the utmost, the highest, and has a correlative in "top-hole." But "ripping"? No one could derive that.

American slang is interesting because it applies and illustrates. One recognises its meaning in a flash of light. Somebody once contraverted the statement that America had no national poetry, by pointing to her slang; and he had reason. American slang very often is poetry, or an admirable substitute for it. It illuminates, synthesises. In England we should fumble for hours to find a swift description of Sir Oliver Lodge; an American looks at him and says "high-brow," and it is done. I was talking a little while ago to the most mercurial and quick-witted comedian on our stage, who had but recently returned from America. Having made an allusion which I, in my slowness, did not at once apprehend, "Ha!" he said, "you're on a freight train!" So I was. In other words, I was behind him in speed; he had employed a recent American phrase to explain delay in the up-take. Americans, however, being very thorough in their neologisms, passengers on freight trains have their chances too; and what I ought to have replied, while puzzling over his first remark, was this: "Snow again, kid. I missed your drift."

Our slang, as I say, seldom describes. Thus, it is rich in terms suggestive of imbecility, but only one has any descriptive merit, and that is "barmy," which means, literally, frothy at the top, yeasty. "Dotty," "up the pole," "cracked," "potty," these are poor, and do not compare with the American "batty" (an abbreviation of "bats in the belfry," which, I believe, our cousins have recently "side-tracked" for "dippy," an inferior word. English slang for the most part is adopted from whimsicality: it is used to give variety to speech, not to supply word-pictures. Fixed rules determine its manufacture, inversion being one of the most common. Thus, a boy arriving at school with the name of White would probably be called Blacky within twenty-four hours. Another rule is association. Thus a boy whose name was Marshall would be called Snelgrove. A third rule is abbreviation, which, operating upon association, would turn Snelgrove to Snell or Snelly in a week. And that would be the end: he would be Snelly for all time to his contemporaries.

On such lines does most English slang run—being rather a supplementary language than an alternative. When young Oxford suddenly began to substitute "er" for the ordinary termination of a word, it was not making slang so much as diversifying and idiotising conversation. Thus a bedmaker was transformed to a "bedder," breakfast to "brekker," and the waste-paper basket, by a desperate effort, became the "wagger pagger bagger" —to be subsequently surpassed when the Prince of Wales arrived at Magdalen, and was known as the "Pragger Wagger": he who only a short time before, at Osborne, on the older principle of inversion, had been called "Sardines." I know a family lost to shame which substitutes the word "horse" for the last syllable of words, and thus removes gravity; and another even more lost where the letter N fitfully takes the place of other initial consonants, so that "a walk in the garden" becomes "a nalk in the narden," also with risible results. But this is not slang. Slang is an alternative word not necessarily descriptive at all but as a rule stronger than the word whose place it takes.

Of all the exasperating forms of speech in which English street humourists indulge, there is none so strange as rhyming slang.

"How's the bother and gawdfers?" I heard a porter in Covent Garden ask, by way of afterthought, loudly of a friend from whom he had just parted. "They're all right," was the shouted reply; and I went on my way in a state of bewilderment as to what they were talking about. What was a bother and what a gawdfer? I could think of nothing except possibly some pet animal, or a nickname for a mutual friend. In a higher commercial rank they might have been gold mines. Among soldiers they would have been officers. I asked a few acquaintances, but without any result, and so made a note of the sentence and dismissed it until the man who knows should arrive.

In course of time I found him.

"What are a bother and a gawdfer?" I asked.

"A wife and kid, of course," he said. ("Of course!" Think of saying "of course" there.)

I looked perplexed, and he added: "Rhyming slang, you know. Wife is 'bother and strife.' Kids are 'God forbids.' And then, according to the rule, the rhyming word is eliminated and the other is the only one used;" and we settled down to discuss this curious development of language and the Londoner's mania for calling nothing by its right name.

When an American is asked a question for which he has no answer, and he says, "Search me," he is emphasising in a striking and humorous way his total lack of information on that point. When he calls a very strong whisky "Tangle-foot," he indicates its peculiar properties in unmistakable fashion in the briefest possible terms. But when a Londoner asks another after his "bother and gawdfers," there may be a certain asinine funniness in the remark, but there is neither cleverness nor colour. He might as well have said "wife and kids," whereas, when Americans use a slang word, it is because it is better than the other word. In American slang every phrase, like the advertisement pictures, "tells a story."

The silliness of rhyming slang is abysmal. Look at this sentence: "So I took a flounder to the pope, laid my lump on the weeping, and did a plough." That is quite a normal remark in any public bar. It means that the speaker went home in a cab and was quickly asleep. Why? Because a cab is a *flounder and dab;* one's home is the *Pope of Rome,* a head is a *lump of lead,* a pillow is a *weeping willow,* and to sleep is to *plough the deep.* A certain bibulous and quarrelsome peer was told by a cabman that he hadn't been "first for a bubble." It was probably only too true; but what do you think it means? It meant that he hadn't been *First of October* for a *bubble and squeak:* reduced to essentials, sober for a week.

All this and more my friend told me. Here are some anatomical terms. The face is the *Chevy,* from *Chevy Chase;* the nose is *I suppose,* this being one of the cases where the whole phrase is always used; the brain is the *once again,* shortened to *once;* the eye is a *mince,* from *mince pie;* the hand is *bag,* from *bag of sand;* the arm the *false,* from *false alarm.* A certain important part of one's anatomy is the *Derby,* or *Derby Kell,* from one Derby Kelly, and the garment that covers it is the *Charlie,* from Charlie Prescott; but who these heroes were I have not discovered. A collar is an *Oxford,* from *Oxford scholar.* Nothing, you see, is gained by rhyming slang; no saving in time; and often indeed the slang term is longer than the real word, as in tie, which is *all me,* from *all me eye,* and *hat,* which is *this and that* in full.

Your feet are your *plates* from *plates of meat;* your boots are your *daisies,* from *daisy roots;* your teeth are your *Hampsteads,* from a north London common; money is *don't be,* from *don't be funny;* the fire is the *Anna,* from *Anna Maria.* Whisky is *I'm so,* from *I'm so frisky;* beer is *pig's ear* in full; the waiter is the *hot,* from *hot pertater;* and so forth.

And these foolish synonyms are really used,

too, as you will find out with the greater ease if (as I did) you loiter in the Dolly. "In the Dolly?" you ask. Oh, if you want any more information let me give it: in the Garden—Covent Garden, from *Dolly Varden.*

But what I want now to know is the extent of the rhyming vocabulary and the process by which new words are added to it. Who invents them and how would they gain currency? That question my friend could not answer.

OF A BONZER AUSTRALIAN POET

AUSTRALIA has its slang too, and some notion of its quality may be obtained, together with a certain play of the emotions, from a little book recently published in Sydney entitled *The Sentimental Bloke,* by C. J. Dennis, which has so authentic a note that I think others may like to know of it too.

The Sentimental Bloke is one Bill, lately a Melbourne crook, but now, through love of Doreen, on the straight. The brief autobiography set out in these fourteen poems relates his loneliness, his meeting with Doreen, his surrender to her charm and the transfiguration of the world in consequence (all the old material, you see; but who wants anything new?), a lover's quarrel, the visit to Doreen's mother, the visit to the clergyman who is to tie the knot, the tying of the knot, the move to the country, and the birth of a son. That is all. But by virtue of truth, simplicity, and very genuine feeling, the result, although the story is related in a difficult argot which usually is anything but lovely, is convincing and often almost too moving to be comfortable. Indeed I know for a certainty that I should avoid any hall where these poems were being recited, not because I should not like to hear them, but because I should not dare. And recited they ought to be: an entertainer with a sympathetic voice and a sense of drama could make his own and Mr. Dennis's fortune by a judicious handling of this book.

Bill meets his fate in the market "inspecting brums at Steeny Isaacs' stall"—a brum being any piece of tawdry finery (from Birmingham).

'Er name's Doreen . . . Well, spare me bloomin' days!
You could er knocked me down wiv arf a brick!
    Yes, me, that kids meself I know their ways,
    An' 'as a name for smoogin' in our click!
I just lines up an' tips the saucy wink.
But strike! The way she piled on dawg! Yer'd think
    A bloke was givin' back-chat to the Queen . . .
        'Er name's Doreen.

Having no luck with Doreen at first, he resorts to guile, and a little later obtains an introduction. A friend having led her up to him:

"This 'ere's Doreen," 'e sez. I sez "Good day."
An', bli'me, I 'ad nothin' more ter say!
    I couldn't speak a word, or meet 'er eye.
    Clean done me block! I never been so shy,
Not since I wus a tiny little cub,
An' run the rabbit to the corner pub—
    Wot time the Summer days wus dry an' 'ot—
        Fer my ole pot.

Me! that 'as barracked tarts, an' torked an' larft,
An' chucked orf at 'em like a phonergraft!
    Gorstrooth! I seemed to lose me pow'r o' speech.
    But 'er! Oh, strike me pink! She is a peach!

Of a Bonzer Australian Poet

The sweetest in the barrer! Spare me days,
I carn't describe that cliner's winnin' ways.
    The way she torks! 'Er lips! 'Er eyes! 'Er hair! . . .
        Oh, gimme air!

. . . .

'Er name's Doreen. . . . An' me—that thort I knoo
    The ways uv tarts, an' all that smoogin' game!
An' so I ort; fer ain't I known a few?
    Yet some'ow . . . I dunno. It ain't the same.
    I carn't tell *wot* it is; but, all I know,
I've dropped me bundle—an' I'm glad it's so.
    Fer when I come to think uv wot I been . . .
        'Er name's Doreen.

Then they walk out together, and one summer night Bill promises her to renounce his old companions:

Fer 'er sweet sake I've gone and chucked it clean:
    The pubs and schools an' all that leery game.
Fer when a bloke 'as come to know Doreen,
        It ain't the same.
There's 'igher things, she sez, for blokes to do,
An' I am 'arf believin' that it's true.

Yes, 'igher things—that wus the way she spoke;
    An' when she looked at me I sorter felt
That bosker feelin' that comes o'er a bloke,
        An' makes 'im melt;
Makes 'im all 'ot to maul 'er, an' to shove
'Is arms about 'er . . . Bli'me? but it's love!

That's wot it is. An' when a man 'as grown
    Like that 'e gets a sorter yearn inside
To be a little 'ero on 'is own;
        An' see the pride
Glow in the eyes of 'er 'e calls 'is queen;
An' 'ear 'er say 'e is a shine champeen.

"I wish't yeh meant it," I can 'car 'er yet,
My bit o' fluff! The moon was shinin' bright,
Turnin' the waves all yeller where it set—
A bonzer night!
The sparklin' sea all sorter gold an' green;
An' on the pier the band—O, 'Ell! . . .Doreen!

Then Doreen insists on his visiting her widowed mother, and after many postponements he does so.

I'd pictered some stern female in a cap
Wot puts the fear o' Gawd into a chap.
An' 'ere she wus, aweepin' in 'er tea
An' drippin' moistcher like a leaky tap.

. . . .

Clobber? Me trosso, 'ead to foot, wus noo—
Got up regardless, fer this interview.
Stiff shirt, a Yankee soot split up the back,
A tie wiv yeller spots an' stripes o' blue.

Me cuffs kep' playin' wiv me nervis fears,
Me patent leathers nearly brought the tears;
An' there I sits wiv, "Yes, mum. Thanks. Indeed?"
Me stand-up collar sorin' orf me ears.

"Life's 'ard," she sez, an' then she brightens up.
"Still, we 'ave alwus 'ad our bite and sup.
Doreen's been *sich* a help; she 'as indeed.
Some more tea, Willy? *'Ave* another cup."

Willy! O, 'Ell! 'Ere wus a flamin' pill!
A moniker that alwus makes me ill.
"If it's the same to you, mum," I replies,
"I answer quicker to the name of Bill."

. . . .

An' then when Mar-in-lor an' me began
To tork of 'ouse'old things an' scheme an' plan,
A sudden thort fair jolts me where I live:
"These is my wimmin folk! An' I'm a man!"

Of a Bonzer Australian Poet

It's wot they calls responsibility.
All of a 'eap that feelin' come to me;
 An' somew'ere in me 'ead I seemed to feel
A sneakin' sort o' wish that I was free.

'Ere's me 'oo never took no 'eed o' life,
Investin' in a mar-in-lor an' wife:
 Some one to battle fer besides meself,
Somethink to love an' shield frum care and strife.

It makes yeh solim when yeh come to think
Wot love and marridge means. Ar, strike me pink!
 It ain't all sighs and kisses. It's yer life.
An' 'ere's me tremblin' on the bloomin' brink.

. . . .

An' as I'm moochin' 'omeward frum the car
A suddin notion stops me wiv a jar—
 Wot if Doreen, I thinks, should grow to be
A fat ole weepin' willer like 'er Mar!

O, 'struth! It won't bear thinkin' of! It's crook!
An' I'm a mean, unfeelin' dawg to look
 At things like that. Doreen's Doreen to me,
The sweetest peach on w'ich a man wus shook.

. . . .

Love is a gamble, an' there ain't no certs.
Some day, I s'pose, I'll git wise to the skirts,
 An' learn to take the bitter wiv the sweet . . .
But, strike me purple! "Willy!" *That's* wot 'urts.

Bill's next ordeal is the interview with the parson:

"Young friend," 'e sez . . . Young friend! Well, spare
 me days!
 Yeh'd think I wus 'is own white-'eaded boy—
The queer ole finger, wiv 'is gentle ways.
 "Young friend," 'e sez, "I wish't yeh bofe great
 joy."

Cloud and Silver

The langwidge that them parson blokes imploy
Fair tickles me. The way 'e bleats an' brays!
"Young friend," 'e sez.

"Young friend," 'e sez . . . Yes, my Doreen an' me
We're gettin' hitched, all straight an' on the square,
Fer when I torked about the registry—
O, 'oly wars! yeh should 'a seen 'er stare;
"The registry?" she sez, "I wouldn't dare!
I know a clergyman we'll go an' see" . . .
"Young friend," 'e sez.

Then the wedding, at which Bill is bewildered by the parson's questions:

"An'—wilt—yeh—take—this—woman—fer—to—be—
Yer—weddid—wife?" . . . O, strike me!
Will I wot?
Take 'er? Doreen? 'E stan's there *arstin'* me!
As if 'e thort per'aps I'd rather not!—

All goes well with the ceremony, partly through the serenity of Doreen and partly through the support of Ginger Mick, the best man; and the bride and bridegroom leave for a honeymoon beside the Bay, jumping into the train at the last moment, and Bill is in a daze of rapture, but comes to himself on hearing the cry "Tickets, please":

You could 'a' outed me right on the spot;
I wus so rattled when that porter spoke.
Fer, 'struth! them tickets I 'ad fair forgot!
But 'e jist laughs, an' takes it fer a joke.
"We must ixcuse," 'e sez, "new-married folk."
An' I pays up, an' grins, an' blushes red . . .

Of a Bonzer Australian Poet

It shows 'ow married life improves a bloke:
If I'd been single I'd 'a' punched 'is 'ead!

Finally the son is born:

Wait? . . . Gawd! . . . I never knoo what waitin' meant
In all me life, till that day I was sent
To loaf around, while there inside—Aw, strike!
I couldn't tell yeh wot that hour was like!

Three times I comes to listen at the door;
Three times I drags meself away once more,
'Arf dead wiv fear; 'arf filled wiv tremblin' joy.
An' then she beckons me, an' sez—"A boy!"

"A boy!" she sez. "An' bofe is doin' well!"
I drops into a chair, an' jist sez—"'Ell!"
It was a pray'r. I feels bofe crook an' glad . . .
An' that's the strength of bein' made a dad.

. . . .

She looks so frail at first, I dursn't stir.
An' then, I leans across an' kisses 'er;
An' all the room gits sorter blurred an' dim . . .
She smiles an' moves 'er 'ead. "Dear lad! Kiss 'im."

Near smothered in a ton of snowy clothes,
First thing, I sees a bunch o' stubby toes,
Bald 'ead, termater face, an' two big eyes.
"Look, Kid," she smiles at me. "Ain't 'e a size?"

'E didn't seem no sorter size to me;
But yet I speak no lie when I agree.
"'E is," I sez, an' smiles back at Doreen.
"The biggest nipper fer 'is age I've seen."

. . . .

But 'struth! 'e is king-pin! The 'ead serang!
I mustn't tramp about, or talk no slang;
I mustn't pinch 'is nose, or make a face,
I mustn't—Strike! 'E seems to own the place!

Cunnin'? Yeh'd think, to look into 'is eyes,
'E knoo the game clean thro'; 'e seems that wise.
    Wiv 'er an' nurse 'e is the leadin' man,
    An' poor ole dad's amongst the "also ran."

"Goog, goo," he sez, an' curls 'is cunnin' toes.
Yeh'd be surprised, the 'eaps o' things 'e knows.
    I'll swear 'e tumbles I'm 'is father, too;
    The way 'e squints at me, and sez "Goog, goo."

. . . .

I think we ort to make 'im something great—
A bookie, or a champeen 'eavy-weight:
    Some callin' that'll give 'im room to spread.
    A fool could see 'e's got a clever 'ead.

. . . .

My wife an' fam'ly! Don't it sound all right!
That's wot I whispers to meself at night.
    Some day, I s'pose, I'll learn to say it loud
    An' careless; kiddin' that I don't feel proud.

My son! . . . If ther's a Gawd 'Oo's leanin' near
To watch our dilly little lives down 'ere,
    'E smiles, I guess, if 'E's a lovin' one—
    Smiles, friendly-like, to 'ear them words—My son.

These few extracts prove not only the sound human character of the book: touches of experiences common to millions of us; but they show also that Mr. Dennis has a mastery of his instrument. In almost no stanza could prose have been more direct, and yet there is music here too, a great command of cadences and a very attractive use of repetition.

And now a word as to Melbourne slang, for some of the phrases in these quotations may not quite tell their own story. With solicitude for his reader Mr. Dennis has provided a very full glossary, from which one gathers that many slang words are common to England, Australia, and America. But Australia has her own too; and none of them quite first-rate, I think. I take them in the order in which they appear above. "Smooging" is billing and cooing; a "click" is a clique or "push," "push" meaning crowd. To "pile on dawg" is to give oneself airs: as we should say, to swank. "Clean done me block!" means flustered, lost one's head. "Running the rabbit" is fetching drink. "Old pot" is old man. A "cliner" is an unmarried young woman. A "tart," in Melbourne, is any young woman, a contraction of "sweetheart." To "drop your bundle" is to surrender, to give up hope. "Leery" is vulgar, low. "Bosher," "boshter," and "bonzer" are adjectives signifying superlative excellence. "Shine" is desirable, and "champeen" a champion.

We now come to the tea-party. "Clobber," of course, is clothes, and "moniker" a name: the East End uses both. To "get wise to the skirts" is to understand women. A "finger" is an eccentric or amusing person. A "king-pin" is a leader. "Dilly" means foolish. Everything else, I think, is clear.

So far I have mentioned only the poems which bear upon the drama of Bill's love and marriage. But there is an account of Day fighting Night, and, later, Night fighting Day, in the manner of the prize ring, which should find a place in any anthology devoted to that rare branch of literature —grotesque in poetry.

OF THE CRUMMLES CODE

ODD books have come my way not infrequently, although never often enough; but rarely has a more curious publication strayed into my hands than the *Theatrical Cipher Code,* compiled and published at Los Angeles, for the benefit of Mr. Crummles when he is in a hurry and in economical mood. Not only is it a strange compilation, supplying a very curious demand; but with its assistance, were I bold enough to use it, which I am not, I could be surrounded, as quickly as an Atlantic liner could bring them, by an army of American entertainers of every description, capable of working every kind of "stunt," singly or in "teams." For example, were I to cable the simple word "Foliage," a "Dutch-Irish team of knockabouts" would be mine. "Foliage" has never meant this to me before; hitherto it has meant the leaves of trees or a volume of poems by Leigh Hunt; but henceforward it will mean a team of Dutch-Irish knockabouts, because that is what this invaluable volume has decreed.

Similarly the word "Follower" means "a fun provoker," and should therefore be a good deal overworked on the wire. Indeed, I wonder that any other word is ever used. A "black face banjo player" is "Focus"; a "clever act" is "Fogless";

a contortionist is "Foist"; a "genuine gilt-edged hit" is "Fomalic"; a "team of skirt dancers able to sing" is "Forcible"; a "pretty girl" is "Fume"; a "Rube act" is "Fungiform"—Rube meaning, in America, rustic, from the fact that out of every ten yokels nine are named Reuben; "Fimble" means "desirable chorus girls," and evidently is not used often enough; "Fixture" means "shapely and good-looking"; "Fitfully" means "not willing to appear in tights"; "Dorsching" is "a leading lady of fine reputation"; "Devolve" means "all our people must be ladies and gentlemen"; "Despond" is "an actor for genteel heavies"; and "Diagrede" is an "encore getter." Let there be more Diagredes, say I, so long as they do not recite patriotic poems or sing sentimental songs.

Only a profound philosopher behind the scenes could have compiled such an exhaustive work as this. Nothing has been forgotten, no contingency overlooked. For example, what do you think "Exhume" means? And I acquit the compiler of any sinister humour in his choice of words, even with the case of "Fitfully," quoted above, to make one doubt it. "Exhume" means "child's mother must accompany," and suggests a thousand complications for the management; and "Excitement" means "child's mother must have transportation on the road and other expenses paid." At the end of most messages the cautious manager will probably add the word "Frantic," meaning "do not want those who cannot deliver the goods," or he may perhaps say "Forester," which means "acts that are not first-class, and as represented, will be closed after the first performance."

So far all has been respectable. Engagements have not necessarily been made, but there has been nothing seamy. The code, however, takes the whole experience of the stage for its province. Thus "Dropwise" means "no contract jumper wanted"; "Dross" means "no drunkards wanted"; "Drove" means "no kickers wanted," a kicker being one who objects to do things outside his own department, an unwilling performer; "Drown" means "no mashers wanted." Some managers apparently do not mind a masher, although they object to a kicker and can put up with a drunkard so long as he does not jump his contract; but for the more fastidious ones who do not want any of the four there is a comprehensive word, "Dropworm," which means "no drunkards, contract-jumpers, kickers, or mashers wanted." Personally, I should use "Dropworm" every time.

The section entitled "Agent to Manager and Manager to Agent" lets a flood of tragic light on touring company life. Thus "Bordering" means "I cannot get out of here until you send me some money." That is from the Agent to the Manager; but quite obviously from Manager to Agent is "Boring," which means, "If you do not sober up at once will discharge you." "Bosom" also must be an unpleasant word to find in a telegram: "Understand you are drinking." On the other hand, what does a Manager say when he receives a telegram with the word "Behalter"—"Our trunks are attached for hotel bills"?

This little book and the demand which led to its supply suggest some of the gigantic ramifications of the business of pleasure. One sees the whole feverish world of entertainers at work so actively as to be unable to write any of its messages in full. The human side of it all is brought out very vividly by this code: the glimpses of stranded mummers in the towns where they did not, as stage folk say, "click"; of desperate managers resorting too often to the grape, or more probably to malt and rye; of anxious performers waiting for telegrams that are to seal their fate, and not knowing the best or worst until it has been de-coded; of noisy braggarts in bars and saloons interrupting each other with tales of personal triumph at Milwaukee, or Duluth; of dejected parties in cheap lodgings hoping for better days. And always one comes back to Crummles; all roads lead to that masterly creation. "The more I read Dickens," said a great writer to me the other day, "the more convinced I am that the Crummles chapters in *Nicholas Nickleby* are the high-water mark of his comic genius." I share this opinion, and this *Theatrical Cipher Code,* though it comes from Los Angeles, whither Mr. Crummles never wandered, is yet full of his brave spirit.

OF ACCURACY

OPENING recently one of the great frivolous illustrated weeklies: those papers in which, by reading from left to right, one identifies footlight favourites and peers' second sons—opening one of these, I came upon a page of ladies of the chorus with whom by a singular chance (for I am not naturally much entangled by the stage) I have some slight acquaintance. For circumstances having conspired to lure me into one of the many avenues which lead to or branch from the Temple of Thespis, I have been much occupied of late in the composition of what with excessive lenience Mr. Crummles calls "lyrics." By this term, which to me has always meant something rather sacred, a joyful or passionate expression of emotion or ecstasy, associated with such names as Shakespeare and Herrick, Shelley and T. E. Brown, Campion and Lovelace, Mr. Crummles means any and every assemblage of words set to music and sung by young ladies to audiences. I never hear my own efforts in this line called lyrics without blushing; but "lyric" being the accepted phrase, just as "comedy," that fine term, is the accepted phrase for all forms of dialogue intended to remove gravity, protest is foolish. Those who are so temerarious as to accept invitations to Rome must adopt Rome's vocabulary. Looking then upon the page of my new friends in the frivolous weekly illustrated paper, I was shocked and horrified to discover that out of some eighteen there portrayed, only a small proportion were accurately named. The names were right, but they were associated with the wrong photographs, or, if you prefer it, the photographs were right, but they were associated with the wrong names.

See how many persons that careless sub-editor has disillusioned by his happy-go-lucky methods! For it is not only I, who do not really matter, but all those dainty-toed, festivous ladies wrongly named who have been rendered sceptical. Rightly named, they would have been plunged into delight, together with their relations, their friends, and their "boys"; but as it is, all these good people are now profoundly impressed by the untrustworthiness of the weekly illustrated press, and in grave doubt as to the bonâ fides of the daily illustrated press too. Imagine the feelings of the mother—or, if you will (for you are so desperately romantic) the fiancé—of Miss Trottie Demury when she (or he) sees under the picture the name of Miss Birdy Dupois. For Miss Demury is beautiful, whereas Miss Dupois —— And then imagine the feelings of the mother or fiancé of Miss Dupois on finding that under her picture is the name of Miss Cussie Roe. For Miss Dupois is beautiful, whereas Miss Roe —— And so it goes on. All these good people are, I say, not only hurt, disappointed, and surprised, but made permanently sceptical.

There is too much unbelief in the world for so many of us thus suddenly to augment the great army of doubt. But how can we help it? Speaking personally, this regrettable occurrence has undermined my confidence not only in that particular number of the paper but in every issue of it that I have ever seen. If on the only occasion when I have special knowledge I am thus deceived, how can I continue to believe in any other statement? All the thrills imparted to me by gazing in earlier numbers on the ivory smile of Miss Dymphna Dent may have been wasted. Those too numerous languorous half-lengths were probably not Mlle. Lala Ratmort at all. Nor am I perhaps acquainted with the lineaments, as I thought I was, of either Count De Spoons, the famous collector of old silver, or Mrs. Debosh-Tinker, the beautiful and popular new hostess. And those fine young fellows who figure week by week in the melancholy Roll of Honour—they may be misnamed too. So you see what it is to have one's faith shattered.

Has any reader of these words, I wonder, ever found perfect accuracy in the newspaper account of any event of which he himself had inside knowledge? Something always is wrong; often, many things are wrong. Where, then, is accuracy to be found? Where is truth? As the modern Pilate might ask, Is there such a thing as truth absolute? Outside the war writings of certain pacifists, which positively crawl with it, I very much doubt if there is.

My experience of truth is that it is granular and not solid; a kind of dust or powder. Every one of us has some grains of it; but some have more than others, and some esteem the material more highly than others. When the Psalmist said "All men are liars," he was understating the case; in his leisure he would have added, "And all men are truth-tellers." It is almost impossible to keep truth out, successfully to suppress it. It crops up everywhere, even in the most unlikely places. Deliberate false witness can be full of it. I believe that every written sentence, every spoken sentence, is almost bound to contain a grain or so, even when the speaker or writer is trying hard to lie; and when the words are spoken in anger, the grains are apt to be numerous. Human nature is so complex and contradictory that practically everything that can be said of any one has some truth in it. But when it comes to truth absolute and unqualified—not Diogenes with a searchlight such as they flash from Hyde Park Corner on the vacant skies could find that.

As one grows older one grows increasingly suspicious, not only of other people's testimony, but of one's own. Memory plays strange and stranger tricks; hearing is less exact; vision becomes defective. Once upon a time I would state a thing with emphasis, and stick to it. Now I state a thing with hesitancy, and when the question, "Are you sure about that?" is put to me, I abandon the position instantly. "No," I say, "I am not sure. I am no longer sure about anything in the world except that death some day is coming."

OF DECEPTION

PASSING through a provincial town recently, I noticed the posters of a touring company who were playing a drama which was a great success a few years ago. The principal part was being taken by a performer of whom, although I keep too many stage names in my memory, I had never before heard, and small portraits of this histrion were to be seen on the hoardings. Underneath these portraits was his name, and underneath his name were the words, in large and arresting letters, "The Leading London Actor." Were one to be asked, apropos of nothing, who is the leading London actor to-day, one would reply—what? Some few years ago the name of that distinguished gentleman who ruled at the Lyceum would naturally have sprung to the lips. But now? Opinions might differ now: they could not have differed then. Anyway, the last name to occur to anybody would be that of the performer on this poster. And yet, if the poster is to be believed, here is the man.

But, you say, the poster is not to be believed: it is only a theatrical advertisement. Subject for thought there! Material for soul-searching on the part of a profession which when prosperity comes to it can take itself seriously indeed. "Only a theatrical advertisement," and therefore—the inevitable corollary runs—not to be swallowed exactly whole. Still, I am not here to moralise Crummles (who, one has to remember, never became Sir Vincent), and, after all, there is no great harm done in foisting one's own valuation of oneself upon the public, since, unless death untimely intervenes, every man finds his true level during his own life. No one would accuse this actor of any criminal wish to deceive; and even if it were criminal, no one would mind, because actors are outside so many laws.

It has been held—and I agree with the saying—that the only person worth deceiving is oneself. So long as one can do that one is happy, because a fool's paradise is, at the time, no worse a paradise than a wise man's, supposing a wise man ever to find one. But to deceive other people and not oneself must be the hollowest of pleasures. It is possible that the profound-looking gentleman in his study, with his head on his hand, in this theatrical poster, really believes himself to be the leading London actor. If so, all I can say is that I envy him his frame of mind. It may be, indeed, that every actor at heart believes himself to be the leading London actor: manqué, perhaps, but still It. It may be that every actress at heart believes herself to be the leading London actress. I hope so, because such self-confidence and self-esteem must be delightful possessions, although their sweetness is, I suppose, impaired by the knowledge that a vindictive or jealous world is fighting successfully against one's genius.

But what of that soldier who recently was sentenced to ten months' imprisonment for obtaining money and hospitality, and even affection, on the strength of a forged Victoria Cross—did he believe his gallant story? He could not have done so; or if he did, then the power of sophistry is vaster even than one imagined. For this fellow himself arranged for the false V.C. to be made and engraved, preparing the inscription himself, and, thus decorated, it was a simple matter in these times to be always surrounded by admirers ready to put their hands in their pockets. If he believed his story, he stands high among the happy self-deluders. If not, I do not envy his thoughts in the small hours when, though at liberty, he could not sleep; nor in his cell.

To put oneself in the place of others is never easy, and it is possible that even Shakespeare did it with less precision than it is customary to think: it may be that his genius over-persuades us of his success. But I imagine that few feats of understanding are more difficult than for one who hates to convey a false impression of himself to get inside the skin of such an impostor as this spurious V.C. I was sorry that the evidence did not bring out more of his real career. He may have not been at the war at all; and, on the other hand, he may have been in the engagement where he claimed to have performed his great deed; and he may actually have performed it, but have done so unobserved, and, therefore, unrewarded; and then in time he may have persuaded himself that he was the victim of oversight, and himself have remedied the omission. Impulsive courage and careful fraud are by no means incompatible. My own feeling, however, is that he was a deliberate fabricator.

The sham hero was deceiving with intent to deceive; the leading London actor, it may be, deceived unconsciously. But sometimes deceit is forced upon us, life being so short, and people so stupid, and iteration so boring. I know that I, for one, who honestly do hate that any false impression of myself should obtain, am frequently misunderstood on the credit side. There is one of my friends, for example, who is firmly convinced that I am an ornithologist. He arrived at this conviction on the strength of a country walk, long ago, in which very insecurely I hazarded the names of certain birds; and nothing can shake him. Many a time have I set him right; but he continues to disbelieve me, and I shall try no more. "Oh, you're too modest," he says with a confident laugh, and there it lies. Were I to die to-morrow and be thought of sufficient interest for an obituary notice, and were this friend invited to contribute to it, he would say something pretty about my wonderful knowledge of bird life. I am certain of this. Others (country walks really are very dangerous) firmly believe that I have profound botanical learning. I have not; but they themselves having none, and I being able to distinguish between a daisy and a blue bell, the fable has grown. I have long since given up disclaiming this too; more probably should I say, "Are you coming out with Linnæus the second?" It is the only way.

As one grows older one grows more hardened, and each year brings a revision of one's code of delicacy. A week or so ago I entered Penzance for the first time, and I had not been there an hour before a policeman saluted me. Were I meticulously honest I should, I suppose, have stopped to inform him that I could not possibly be the person he had thought I was, and in a sense have returned him his gesture of honour; but I did not. I merely acknowledged his courtesy, and fortified him in his delusion either that he had seen me before or that I was somebody of importance.

OF PLANS FOR ONE MORE SPRING

(February 1915)

IT is much on my mind just now that I must not waste a minute of the spring that is coming. We have waited for it longer than for any before, and the world has grown so strange and unlovely since spring was here last. Life has become so cheap, human nature has become so cruel and wanton, that all sense of security has gone. Hence this spring must be lived, every moment of it.

I know it is coming, for I had a sudden foretaste this morning. I was conscious of it stirring beneath the mould; I could hear it and feel it. Moreover, the birds have begun to make sleep difficult after six, bless their throats! The thrushes (the darlings!) have begun to perch on the topmost spray of the yew tree to try their voices. Soon the starlings will be scrabbling at the eaves as early as five, confound them!

Every year I determine to do certain things in the spring. This year I must surely do them. There is a hedge, I know, in a meadow, under which one finds white violets. I must go there. Daffodils, too. I know of four certain spots for daffodils; not the splendid yellow lilies (as they can grow to be) of the London shops—the stately and distinguished "Sir Watkin Wynn" and so forth—but the daffodils of the meadows, short and sturdy, fluttering in the winds of March, all bending their lovely heads together. One at least—and I hope two—of those spots I shall visit.

I shall find my first primroses on the banks of a stream about two miles away. And one day I must do a little gardening—not because I like digging, for I detest it more almost than any form of exercise, except rowing—but in order (*a*) to get the smell of the earth, and (*b*) to be in the company of a robin once more. No other toil, I have observed, so bridges the gulf fixed by the All-Wise between man and robins as digging—turning over the soil. Chopping wood is not bad; but digging is best. I know that after two minutes of spade-work a robin will arrive on the scene and establish himself in the stalls, so to speak. Where he comes from will be one mystery, and how he learnt that I am there will be another. But he will arrive; the marconigraph of the birds will be in action; their spy system will again do its work.

There is a copse which the woodmen have been clearing this winter. You know, of course, what this means. It means that in May the bluebells will flood it like an azure sea. Not that I shall wait until May to go there, for the anemones come first, and the primroses, and now and then an early thrush flies scolding from her nest among the faggots; but it is going to be the best bluebell site about here.

I know a cowslip field too. There is no need to pick any of the other flowers except the violets; all the others are more satisfying as they grow. But cowslips must be picked. You pick them until you have a big enough bunch to bury your face in. Then you bury your face in it. That is one of the rules of spring, and if ever it was broken, it shall not be this year.

And I must see about erecting the owl box at once, because I can think of nothing more fascinating than to have a family of owls growing up close to the house, and to watch their ghostly parents conveying food to them. I do not say, of course, that a pair of owls will come merely because a home is provided; but they may. Anyway, it must not be my fault that they do not.

And the walks I shall take! That one up the bostel at the side of Fronbury, and then along the turf among the larks for three miles, and then winding down through the beech woods (with the tenderest green on them you ever saw) to the village of East Tritley. (These are not the real names. It is hardly likely that I should give the real names: I don't want half London down here!) At East Tritley right under the down lives a friend in a Tudor manor-house, with a formal garden and wainscoting, a picture by Matthew Maris, and other delectabilities, and with him I shall have tea, and saunter slowly back just as the day is turning to evening and the thrushes and blackbirds are at their best. And as I draw near home I shall walk into the evening turmoil of the rookery close by. This racket, as a matter of fact, has already begun, but at present it is the usual row between builders and architects over the specifications. Later there will be the jangle of the family too.

The great charm of this walk is the wide prospect from the top of the downs—some nine hundred feet up—and then the search, as one descends to the plain at the foot, for the boldest primrose: that is to say, for that primrose which has succeeded in climbing highest up the slopes. Incidentally, there will be hawks to watch. Now and then I shall almost step on a hare in her form. Also, there is a bank on the north side of Fronbury, where, if the sun is hot, one is almost sure to see an adder or two, and perhaps a grass snake, thawing the winter from their bones.

Another walk will be through Tritley Park, among the venerable Spanish chestnuts and the deer, to Vests Common, where another friend has what the cultured call a pied-à-terre and the simple a cottage. The special charm of Vests is that it is an oasis of red sand in a district mainly composed of clay or chalk. Scotch firs and other firs are the only trees, save for delicate silver birches which in the spring are like green flames; and in May the brake ferns begin to force their arched necks through the peat like submerged swans. Well, Vests Common will be a very constant joy to me this spring. I shall roam there continually, and, very likely, induce my friend to let me have his cottage for a few days directly the nightingales are in force.

What a programme!

"R.C."

THE letters at the head of this essay do not refer to any royal college, or to the late Lord Randolph Churchill, or to "Randall Cantuar" (as the Archbishop of Canterbury humorously signs himself), or to that comforting form of religion as dispensed by his great rival the Pope. They were copied from a Continental Bradshaw, where you find them or not, according as to whether or not a train has a Restaurant Car attached to it. They stand for Restaurant Cars, those structures of brown wood and plate-glass which trains in Europe mysteriously pick up and attach to themselves at odd places en route, and again, their mission of more or less nourishing the traveller fulfilled, as mysteriously shed.

To Americans I suppose it is nothing to eat at a table on a train. But in England there are still millions of people who have never in their own country partaken of food on railway journeys except from nose-bags, and have never crossed the Channel. There are also a certain number, both English and Americans, who know the European Restaurant Car intimately, and deem the time spent within it the best part of the journey; and there are those who detest it. Of the latter am I.

When the indictment of the Wagon-lit Restaurant Cars comes to be drawn up, I shall be able to assist very materially. To begin with, there is that offensive autocracy on the part of the attendant which determines where you are to sit, a matter that is much to you and nothing to him, and yet upon which he is absolute and uncompromising. Never has any one yet, taking a seat independently, been permitted to retain it. Secondly, there is the considerable item of ventilation, no middle way being possible between the two extremes of suffocating heat and a draught that may leave a hundred bitter legacies. I say nothing of the discomforts caused by the oscillation of the train, through which you pour your wine into your neighbour's glass, for that obviously is less the fault of the wagon-lit than of the track-layer (there is one point between Calais and Boulogne where every bottle crashes on its side); nor is it exactly the car's fault that the people who sit opposite you are not only always profoundly and minutely antipathetic, but are so secretive with the salt.

We pass on then to more personal charges, such as the wine, which is always very bad and very dear; and the utensils, which those who know may be seen polishing afresh with their napkins (so that it has become a sign of much travel when a man does this); and thus we reach the meal itself. Here again the caprice of the attendants is more marked, a certain type of man always having a full selection of hors d'œuvres set before him, including butter, while another group, of which I am a birth-right member, is put off with only one or at most two varieties, and those unpalatable. I have spent more pains to get the butter in a Restaurant Car than other men in acquiring virtue; but enough indigestible radishes have surrounded me to sustain Mr. Bernard Shaw's remarkable genius for a week, and enough tessellated sausage to pave a bathroom. With the rest of the meal it is the same—not only do I dislike the food, but others get more than I. Some travellers who seem to possess many of the stigmata of the gentleman are able even to ask for a second helping. That these men fill me with a kind of perverted admiration I will not deny, but I cannot imitate them. I cannot interrupt a wagon-lit waiter in what seems to be as much a natural and irresistible process as the onrush of water at Niagara. I have not that courage, that self-assertiveness. Nor do I care enough.

And then the delays between the courses; the injustices of the distribution, by which the same table again and again gets the first chance at the new dish; the strain of the noise of it all, aggravated by the anxiety that one feels when a waiter lurches along balancing a thousand plates at once —such are a few only of the damaging criticisms which I am prepared to bring against the Restaurant Car.

But (such is the sharpness of the serpent's tooth) do you suppose for an instant that any single one of these charges would be endorsed by the small person of comparatively tender years, now at school, whom it is my quaint fortune to call daughter and have to clothe and support? Not one. Anything less filial than she would become if she were asked to back me in the matter could not be imagined. For to her the Wagon-lit Restaurant Car is the true earthly paradise, and travel on the Continent merely a means of gratifying her passion for eating on trains. Her expression of joy on taking what in such places they call a seat, a stubborn, resisting, struggling thing which has to be held down by main force before you can occupy it, is amazing. Her happy excitement on reading the menu and finding the same tiresome dishes is incredible. Her delight in every moment of the meal is my despair. But no reverses can change her, and if she asks how long does it take to get from Paris to Rome, and after working out the journey with infinite trouble I tell her, it is only that she may compute the number of wagon-lit lunches and dinners that will fall to her ecstatic lot. She even likes the ice-pudding; she even likes her neighbours.

As a fond father, I say, then, let the Restaurant Cars go on. But when peace returns, and Europe is again unlocked, and I travel once more (as in the Golden Age) from Calais or Boulogne to Paris, if I am alone I shall again provide myself with the basket from the buffet which contains half a chicken and half a bottle of claret and a tiny corkscrew and an apple or a pear and bread and butter and a piece of Gruyère and a paper napkin, and eat it in seclusion in a compartment which the other people have left in order that they may avoid each other's eyes, and be balked of sufficient nourishment, amid all the clatter and nervousness of the Restaurant Car.

THE TWO LADIES

AFTER reading aloud some of the sketches by The Two Ladies (as I always think of "Martin Ross" and Miss E. Œ. Somerville), and in particular "The House of Fahy," which I have always held is one of the best short stories ever written, with a last sentence that no one but a professional elocutionist with nerves of steel could possibly compass, it amused me to imagine a room filled with devotees of the *Experiences of an Irish R.M.*, such as might as easily exist as a Boz Club, capping quotations from that and its companion books and finding pleasure in expressing admiration in the warmest terms and in minute detail; and there are not many pleasures greater than that.

The discussion might, indeed, have begun by the old question, What are the best short stories in the world? and my own insistence on the claims of this very "House of Fahy" to a place high on the list; because, as I should have urged, it relates an episode proper only to the short-story medium; there is no word too many or too few; it has atmosphere and character; it is absorbing; it has a beginning, a middle, and an end—such an end!

"But what about 'The Maroan Pony'?" some one might have inquired. "Isn't that a perfect short story too?"

And I should have replied that it is.

"And 'Harrington's'?" some one else might have urged. "Isn't that perfect? And it has an extra quality, for in addition to all the humour of it, and the wonderful picture of a country auction sale, it has that tragic touch. To my mind it is greater than 'The House of Fahy.'"

And then I am sure that a most emphatic claim for "Trinket's Colt" as the best of all would have been formulated; and by this time we should have been right in the thick of it, all eager to speak and be heard.

To me The Two Ladies have long been the only contemporary authors whom it is absolutely necessary to read twice instantly: the first time for the story itself, which is always so intriguing—and the more so as you get more familiar with the ingenuity of their methods—as to exact a high speed; and the second time for the detail, the little touches of observation and experience, and the amazing, and to an envious writer despairful, adequacy of epithet. And having read them twice, I find that whenever I pick them up again there is something new, something not fully tasted before. Indeed, at any rate in the *R.M.* series, they are the most trustworthy and re-readable of any writers of our time.

"Talking of observation and experience" (here I resume the report of the imaginary club of devotees), one said, "they know everything. That they should be wise about hunting and Irish life is natural. Hunting and Irish life are their strong suit. But they know all about the sea too: no one has so etched in the horrors of a ground swell on a hot day. They know all about servants. They know all about dogs—what dogs think and how dogs feel."

"But most remarkable of all," said another, "is their knowledge of man—and married man at that. Who would ever have guessed that Major Sinclair Yeates was the invention of two single women? I cannot find a single slip into sheer femininity in all his narratives."

The superiority of the *R.M.* stories over the others would have given us a wide field for debate; and I should certainly have cited their fellow-countryman Goldsmith as an earlier example of the greater ease and power that some authors attain when they assume an imaginary character. For good as their other sketches and novels are, The Two Ladies were never so fully armed at every point as when they thought themselves Major Yeates—just as Goldsmith was so much more effective when he was the Vicar of Wakefield or the Citizen of the World.

"It is possible," I might have said, "that all collaborators should invent some such personality as the Major, to give them common ground on to which they can simultaneously step." And the case of Addison and Steele and Sir Roger, although there was there no impersonation, would perhaps have occurred to me.

Thus we might have begun, and so have passed on to the consideration of the work of The Two

Ladies as a whole, and have grown happy in the excitement of bestowing praise.

"They are the only humourists," I seem to hear another saying, "who never relax. In the *R.M.* books their whole attitude to life is humorous, and so splendid is their sense of duty to their readers, that their almost every sentence is humorous. Do you remember, for example, how when Anthony asks his mother what auctions are, that confirmed bargain-seeker does not merely tell him, as another author might have made her, but 'instructs him even as the maternal carnivore instructs her young in the art of slaughter'? And how Flurry's handwriting was 'an unattractive blend of the laundress's bill and the rambling zigzag of the temperature charts'?"

"If you are going to begin quoting good phrases," I should have said, "I can give you plenty. For I have always held that when it comes to sheer writing, good writing, clear writing, vivid writing, vigilant writing, The Two Ladies have no equal and no superior. The art of suggesting one effect by a reference to another was never practised with finer skill than by these authors. Do you remember how when the two terriers followed Flurry's hunt, their 'yelps streamed back from them like the sparks from an engine'? and the uneven Irish road which 'accepted pessimistically the facts of Nature'? and the reluctant dog who 'resolved himself into jelly and lead'? and how when the R.M. was told by Flurry to watch a certain spot for the fox, the concentration of his eyeglass upon the gap was of 'such intensity that had the fox appeared he would have fallen into a hypnotic trance'?"

"A remarkable thing in their writing," another might say, "is their double gift of painting with equal power broad landscape and Dutch interiors. Some of their rapid Irish backgrounds are marvels of lucid impressionism, and never a word more of it than the story requires. Their instinct for saliences in landscape and in all their descriptions is indeed marvellous."

"And their knowledge of their countrymen!" he might continue. "Do you remember how they refer to an Irishman as always a critic in the stalls and yet in spirit behind the scenes too? And their Irish idioms! The whisky that was 'pliable as milk'!"

"Another remarkable thing about them," I hope I should have dropped in, "is what one might call their all-of-a-pieceness. Their first story and their last are equally mellow and mature, although years intervened. They forget nothing. The *R.M.* remains the same."

"And their modesty! They have added to fiction certain characters that will not die for generations and may even be immortal—in Flurry Knox, in his grandmother, in Slipper, in Maria, in Dr. Jerome Hickey—and there has been no flourish of trumpets, no heralding. These figures have not even had a novel to appear in, but occur casually in that previously most negligible literary form—the humorous sketch of Irish life. The Real

Charlotte, that wonderful creation, it is true, has a long novel all to herself; but for one reader fortunate enough to know her, there are fifty who know the others."

Finally might come this comment: "They are the last really passionate friends of the noble animal. Not that they don't understand motor-cars; but their attitude to horses is more than understanding: it is intimate, sympathetic, humorous, with a vast tolerance for equine mischief. Do you remember the trainer of Fanny Fitz's 'Gamble' in *All on the Irish Shore*—how he met a mare he had once owned, and he did not know her but she knew him? It is one of the prettiest pieces of writing that ever came out of Ireland. It was after the fair at Enniscar, 'an' I was talking to a man an' was coming down Dangan Hill, and what was in it but herself [the mare] coming up in a cart! An' I didn't look at her good nor bad, nor know her, but sorra bit but she knew me talking, an' she turned into me with the cart. "Ho! ho! ho!" says she, an' she stuck her nose into me like she'd be kissing me. Be dam, but I had to cry. An' the world wouldn't stir her o' that till I'd lead her on meself.' And then he utters this immortal sentiment: 'As for cow nor dog nor any other thing, there's nothing would rise your heart like a horse.'—Isn't that beautiful?"

Thus enthusiastically might we have talked!

And now the bond has snapped, and "Martin Ross," who was Miss Violet Martin, is dead. With her death the series stops, for though neither was the dominant spirit, the prosperity of the work demanded both. As to The Two Ladies' method of collaboration I know nothing, and should like to know all; which held the pen I have no notion, or if one alone held it. But that it was complete and perfect is proved by this sentence from a private letter from one very near to them, which I may perhaps take the liberty of quoting, since it embodies a remark made by the survivor of the many, many years' partnership. "There isn't a page, there isn't a paragraph, there isn't a line which either of us could claim as her sole work." That is collaboration in the highest degree, two minds that not only work as one, but are one.

ONCE UPON A TIME

I The Two Perfumes

ONCE upon a time there was a common, and on it a cottage had been built with a high bank beside it, and on this bank grew a lilac-tree whose branches hung very near the path, and below the lilac was a great mass of rich brown wallflowers.

Looking up one afternoon the lilac saw a wayfarer approaching. "I hope he will notice me and stop," she thought; for she had but a short time of blossom, and she knew it, and it gave her pleasure to be courted and praised.

"There's some one coming," she said to the wallflower. "He looks rather interesting. I think he'll stop."

"If he does," said the wallflower, "it will be for you. I've been going on too long. They're all tired of me by now."

"I don't agree with you," said the lilac. "I wish I did. This one looks to me as if he would be fond of both of us. I tell you he's nice."

"Let's have a bet," said the wallflower. "I bet you that he pays more attention to you than to me."

"Very well," said the lilac; "and I bet he pays more attention to you. How much?"

"Two bees," said the wallflower.

"Done," said the lilac as the man reached them.

He was a middle-aged man, with a kindly face, and he knelt down by the wallflowers and took a long draught of them.

Immediately his years left him and he was a boy again. He thought himself in an old garden. The walls had toad-flax between the bricks. There was a tortoise in the greenhouse. The lawn was very bare where he and his brothers and sisters played too much cricket. All along the front of the house was a bed of wallflowers, and in a chair by the window of the dining-room lay a lady sewing. Every now and then she looked up and smiled at the cricketers. "Well hit!" she would say, or "Well caught!"

Whenever they were out they ran to her for a second and kissed her—not long enough to interrupt the game, but just to let her know that she was the most beautiful and adorable creature in the world.

The man's eyes filled with tears. Why did the scent of wallflowers always bring back this scene, and this only? But it did.

He reached up and pulled a branch of lilac to his face, and straightway he was a young man again. He was not alone. It was night and the moon was shining, and he was standing in the garden with a beautiful girl beside him. It was the hour of his betrothal. "How wonderful!"

she said at last. "Oh, I am too happy!" And again his eyes filled with tears.

Then once more he buried his face in the wall-flowers. . . .

After he had passed on his way across the common, "I've won," said the lilac sadly.

"Yes," said the wallflower. "I owe you two bees. I won't forget to send them on."

II The Dog Violets

Once upon a time there was a patch of dog violets growing on a bank in March. They were very beautiful but they had no scent, and the country people, knowing this, passed them by.

Day after day the flowers heard scornful remarks about themselves. "They're only dog violets," said one of the knowing country people. "Don't bother about them," said another. "I know where there's real violets," said a third; "come on!"

And since no one likes to be overlooked and despised, even though attention should mean destruction, the dog violets were very unhappy. "As if perfume was everything!" they said; while one of them went so far as to declare that she always found the scent of the other kind of violets overpowering. "A strong scent is so vulgar," she added. "Yes," said another, "and so are rich colours. Pale tints are much more distinguished."

One day the princess came driving along from

the royal city in her gold coach, and seeing the patch of flowers on the bank she gave orders for the carriage to stop. "Oh, how beautiful!" she said, for, being a princess, she had never seen violets growing before; she had seen only tiger-lilies and camellias and smilax and Maréchal Niels. "How beautiful!" she cried, and she bade her lord chamberlain bring her a great bunch.

"Those!" he replied in surprise. "Does not your Royal Highness know that they are only dog violets; they have no scent."

"The darlings!" she cried. "It wouldn't matter if they had, I've got such an awful cold;" and she pressed them to her white bosom, where in an ineffable rapture of pride and content they swooned away.

III The Devout Lover

Once upon a time there was a fox who fell in love with a pretty little lady fox. He called her either Sweet Auburn or Loveliest Vixen of the Plain, and in the small hours, when all the world was asleep, they went for delightful strolls together, and talked a deal of pleasant nonsense, and killed numbers of young chickens, and fed each other with titbits, as lovers do.

One day Sweet Auburn casually mentioned her approaching birthday, which chanced to be on May the 15th, and said she would like nothing so much as gloves.

"What colour?" he asked.

"Purple," she told him; and he agreed.

"With white and purple spots inside," she added; and he agreed again.

"And lined with glistening hairs," she called after him; and he agreed once more.

When, however, he told his mother, the old lady was discouraging. "They won't be out by then," she said, "fox-gloves won't."

His mother was a widow. An unfortunate meeting with the local pack had deprived her for ever of her beloved chicken-winner. She had however brought up, with much pluck and resource, her family, unaided.

"You'll never get them by the 15th," she added, "that's a fortnight too early."

"But I must," replied her son, with the impetuosity and determination of youth.

"You'll never," said his mother.

Undismayed he set forth and searched the country-side for fox-gloves. He found many plants in various early stages of growth, but all were far indeed from the time to exhibit their stock-in-trade.

"What did I tell you?" said his mother.

The day drew nearer. He extended his travels, but in vain, until one morning, at about a quarter to five, when he ought to have been at home again, he came upon a fox-glove stalk which actually had buds on it. Carefully marking the spot, he rushed back with the news.

"But how can blossoms be ready in four days?" he asked his mother.

"Intensive culture," said the old lady. "There's nothing but that."

"I don't know what you mean," said her son.

"Of course not; you're only a child. It means you must supply heat and nourishment. You must curl your warm body round that stalk every evening as soon as the sun sets and lie there without moving till the sun's up, and you must water the roots with your tears. On no account must you move or nap."

"Really?" he asked nervously.

"If you truly love," said his mother.

"I wonder," he thought; but after paying another visit to Sweet Auburn he knew that he did, and he promised her the gloves for a certainty.

Late on the evening of the 15th, when she had almost given him up, he staggered into her abode, wan and weary, and laid a pair of superb gloves at her feet. They were a beautiful purple lined with glistening hairs and they had white and purple spots inside.

"Many happy returns," he said. "They're absolutely the first of the season. You'll be able to set the fashion."

"Darling Reynolds!" she replied, embracing him, and named the happy day.

IV Wireless

Once upon a time there was a daisy who conceived a fierce passion for another daisy a few inches away. He would look at this daisy hour after hour with mute longing. It was impossible to tell his love, because she was too far off, for daisies have absurdly weak voices. They have eyes of gold and the most dazzling linen, but their voices are ridiculous.

One day by happy chance a bronze-wing butterfly flitted into the meadow, and the daisy saw it passing from one to another of his companions, settling for a few moments on each. Bronze-wings are partial to daisies. He was an ingenious and enterprising fellow, this flower—something, in fact, of a "Card," as they say in the Five Fields —and an idea suddenly came to him which not only would enable his dearest wish to be realised but might be profitable too.

It was an idea, however, that could be carried out only with the assistance of the bronze-wing, and he trembled with anxiety and apprehension lest the butterfly should pass him by.

At last, however, after half a dozen false approaches which nearly reduced the daisy to the trembling condition of an anemone, the bronze-wing settled right on his head.

"Good afternoon," said the daisy. "You're just the person I wanted to see."

"Good afternoon," said the bronze-wing. "What can I do for you?"

"Well," said the daisy, "the fact is I have a message for a lady over there. Would you take it?"

"With pleasure," said the bronze-wing; and the daisy whispered a loving message to him.

"Which one is it?" he asked, when ready to start.

"How can you ask? Why, the beautiful one," said the daisy.

"They all look alike to me," said the bronze-wing.

"Foolish myope," said the daisy. "There's only one really beautiful one—just over there."

"All right," said the bronze-wing; "but you mustn't call me names," and off he flitted.

Presently he came back and whispered the reply, which was so satisfactory that the edge of the daisy's dazzling white ruff turned pink.

"Now," said the bronze-wing, "what about my payment?"

"Well," said the daisy, "my idea is that you should devote yourself wholly to this meadow and the daisies in it. There are enough of us to keep you going. You won't have to travel and get tired, and you'll be safe because no boys with butterfly nets"—the bronze-wing shuddered—"have ever been seen here. You will become our Mercury and keep us all in communication. And in return——"

"Yes?" said the bronze-wing eagerly.

"In return we will refuse the attentions of other visitors; all our honey shall be for you. All our energies shall go to providing you with the best."

"Done," said the bronze-wing.

"Better make a start at once," said the Card. "Here's another message for that lady;" and he whispered again, and off the bronze-wing flitted.

He was soon back with the reply, which turned the edges of the daisy's ruff pinker than before.

"Now tell her this," said the daisy.

"But what about the rest of the field?" asked the bronze-wing.

"Never mind about any one else," said the lover.

V The Vaseful

Once upon a time a little company of the wild flowers of spring found themselves together in a vase. It was the first time that many of them had met; for although they came from the same district, indeed the same copse, and had heard of each other's characteristics, they had grown up too far away from each other for conversation, and flowers, of course, cannot walk. It was therefore with peculiar interest that they now examined each other and fell a-talking.

There was naturally a little reserve at first, for social grades must be preserved; but they were so tightly packed in the vase, and for the most part so forlorn at their fate, that barriers soon disappeared, and the oxlip ceased to despise the cowslip, and the cowslip was quite nice to the primrose, and the purple orchis almost dropped his aristocratic drawl when talking to the bluebell.

The purple orchis, who was not only a heavy drinker but rather a bully, was the only one who was not unhappy to be there. "I knew I should attract attention soon," he said; "there were so few of us and we're so noticeable. By Jove, this tipple's delicious!" and he took a long draught.

"Please don't push so," said a small voice at his side.

"Why, what's the matter?" the orchis asked. "You anemones are always such weaklings."

"I'm afraid I feel rather faint," replied the anemone. "I'm not strong at any time, it's true, and just now, no matter how I stretch, I can't quite reach the water. I'm afraid that little girl put me in the vase rather carelessly."

"Or else"—the orchis laughed—"or else I'm getting more than my share. Ha, ha!"

"Surely," said a cowslip to a bluebell, "there were more of you in the little girl's hands when we left the wood?"

"Alas, yes," said the bluebell. "Most of my closest friends were picked too, and I hoped we were all coming along together. But for some reason or other which has never been explained to me bluebells seem to be more easily and more often thrown away after being picked than any other flower; and all my companions must have suffered that fate."

"It is quite true," said the cowslip. "From my high position on the bank I have again and again seen bunches of bluebells forsaken by children. How is it, I wonder? It is not as if they were ugly; although blue is not every one's colour."

"Perhaps," said the cuckoo-spit with a touch

of sarcasm, for he disliked the cowslip, "it's because you can't make tea of them."

"No," said the oxlip, who was looked up to as something of a sage by reason of his strength and his many eyes, "it is because bluebells are so much more beautiful when they are in a wood among greenery than when they are packed together in a human hand, and the human hand suddenly realises this and drops them in disappointment."

"Thank you," said the bluebell with a sigh of content.

"The wonder," the oxlip continued with a glance at the cuckoo-spit, "is that some flowers are ever picked at all."

Silence followed, broken by a little sigh. It was the dying anemone's last breath.

VI Ups and Downs

Once upon a time towards the end of June the birds gathered together to compare notes as to the nesting season. It is a regular habit—a kind of stock-taking.

"And what has been your luck?" the owl asked the plover.

"Half and half," said the plover. "My first clutch of eggs—beauties they were, too—were found by a farm boy, and within a couple of days they were being devoured by a pretty actress, at one-and-six apiece; but I need hardly say," added the plover with a wink, "that it was not the little lady herself who paid for them.

"So I laid again," the plover continued, "and this time we pulled through; and this very morning I've been giving my family a lesson in taking cover. The difficulty is to make them keep their silly little beaks shut when they're in danger: they will *cheep* so, and that, of course, gives the show away. Still, chicks will be chicks, you know."

"Yes indeed," replied the owl; "but years will put that right only too successfully;" and both birds sighed.

"Yes," said the nightingale to the woodpecker, "I managed capitally. I had a wonderful season. Every night people came to hear me sing; Caruso couldn't have more devoted audiences. We brought up a healthy family, too, with strong musical tendencies. In fact, it wasn't till yesterday that anything went wrong; and that wasn't exactly a calamity, although it hurt me quite a little bit."

"Tell me," said the woodpecker.

"With pleasure," said the nightingale. "It was like this: I flew from the hedge just as that nice lady at the Grange came along with her little girl, and the little girl saw me and, as children always do,—you've all heard them time and again,—asked the mother what that pretty brown bird was called. Now this, you must understand, is the lady who has been leaning out of her window every night all through June just to hear me sing; she has even written a poem to me; but what do you think she said to the little girl in reply? 'That brown bird, darling? That's only a sparrow.' "

"You've been as immoral as usual, I suppose?" said the thrush to the cuckoo.

"Quite," said the cuckoo, "if by immorality you mean taking furnished lodgings for my family instead of going in for small ownership, like you."

"That's not wholly what I meant," said the thrush. "There's such a thing as taking furnished apartments and paying for them, and there's such another thing as depositing your family there and never showing up again."

"Still," said the cuckoo, "it's a very small family—only one. I never deposit more than one egg in each nest."

"I wish, all the same," said the thrush, "you'd tell me why you are so averse from erecting a home of your own."

"I don't exactly know," said the cuckoo, "but I think it's fastidiousness. I never can find a site to suit me. Either there's no view, or the water's bad, or I dislike the neighbours; try as I will, I never can settle. So there you are!"

"And who, may I ask," said the thrush, "has had the honour of foster-mothering your illustrious offspring this season?"

"I selected nuthatches," said the cuckoo; "and they weren't half disagreeable about it either. While as for their own children, the little pigs, they couldn't have taken it with less philosophy. Grumbled day and night. My poor darlings were jolly glad when they were fledged, I can tell you."

"What are you going to do with them?" the thrush asked.

"I haven't made up my mind," said the cuckoo. "What do you advise?"

"Apprentice them to a builder," said the thrush as he flew away.

VII The Alien

Once upon a time a poet was sitting at his desk in his cottage near the woods, trying to write.

It was a hot summer day and great fat white clouds were sailing across the sky. He knew that outdoors was best, but still he dutifully sat on, pen in hand, trying to write.

Suddenly, among all the other sounds of busy urgent life that were filling the warm sweet air, he heard the new and unaccustomed song of a bird: new and unaccustomed, that is to say, there, in that sylvan retreat. The notes poured out, now shrill, now mellow, now bubbling like musical water, but always rich with the joy of life, the fulness of happiness. Where had he heard it before? What bird could it be?

Hastening out with his field-glasses, he tracked the sound to a group of elm trees from which proceeded sweeter and more tumultuously exultant song than they had ever known; and after a while he discerned among the million leaves a little yellow bird, with its throat trembling with rapture.

But the poet was not the only one who had heard the strange melody.

Once Upon a Time

"I say," said a chaffinch to a sparrow, "did you hear that?"

"What?" inquired the sparrow, who was busy collecting food for a very greedy family.

"Why, listen!" said the chaffinch.

"Bless my soul," said the sparrow, "I never heard that before."

"It's a strange bird," said the chaffinch; "I've seen it. All yellow."

"All yellow?" said the sparrow. "What awful cheek!"

"Yes, isn't it?" replied the chaffinch. "Can you understand what it says?"

"Not a note," said the sparrow. "Another of those foreigners, I suppose. We shan't have a tree to call our own soon."

"That's so," said the chaffinch. "There's no end to them. Nightingales are bad enough, grumbling all night; but when it comes to yellow birds—well."

"Hello," said a passing tit, "what's the trouble now?"

"Listen!" said the others.

The tit was all attention for a minute while the gay triumphant song went on.

"Well," he said, "that's a rum go. Novel, I call it. What is it?"

"It's a yellow foreigner," said the chaffinch.

"What's to be done with it?" the tit asked.

"There's only one thing for self-respecting British birds to do," said the chaffinch. "Stop it."

"Absolutely," said the tit. "I'll go and find some others."

"Yes, so will we," said the chaffinch; and off they all flew, full of righteous purpose.

Meanwhile the canary sang on and on, and the poet at the foot of the elm listened with delight.

Suddenly, however, he was conscious of a new sound, a noisy chirping and harsh squawking which seemed to fill the air, and then a great cloud of small angry birds assailed the tree. For a while the uproar was immense; and then, out of the heart of the tumult, pursued almost to the ground where the poet stood, fell the body of a little yellow bird, pecked to death by a thousand avenging furies.

Seeing the poet, they made off in a pack, still shrilling and squawking, conscious of the highest rectitude.

The poet picked up the poor mutilated body. It was still warm and it twitched a little, but never could its life and music return.

While he stood thoughtfully there an old woman, holding an open cage and followed by half a dozen children, hobbled along the path.

"My canary got away," she said. "Have you seen it? It flew in this direction."

"I'm afraid I have seen it," said the poet, and he opened his hand.

"My little pet!" said the old woman. "It sang so beautifully, and it used to feed from my fingers. My little pet."

The poet returned to his work. "'In tooth and claw,'" he muttered to himself.

VIII Breathing Space

Once upon a time there was an old pheasant—a real veteran who had come victorious out of many battues. Not perhaps wholly unscathed, for his tail was no longer the streaming meteoric plume that it once had been, but sound in wind and limb.

No one knew his lordship's guests so well as he, so often had he seen them in the coverts: old Sir Mark, who had an arm-chair at the angle of the two best drives; Sir Humphry, with his eternal cigarette in the long gold tube; the red-faced Colonel, who always shot too late; the purple-faced Major, who always shot too soon; the smiling agent, who would so tactfully disown a bird whenever it seemed politic; and all the rest of them.

How the veteran rocketer had escaped I cannot say, but shoot after shoot found him still robust and elusive, while his relations were falling all around, some, to their dying satisfaction, thudding into the features of their assassins.

One morning three young pheasants came flying up to this Nestor in a state of nervous excitement.

"Quick! quick!" they said, "the gentlemen are leaving the Hall. Tell us where to go to be safe."

"Go?" said the old bird. "Don't go anywhere. Stay where you are."

"But they're coming this way," said the young pheasants.

"Let them come," said the old bird. "There's no danger. Why don't you use your ears?"

"What do you mean?" they asked.

"Listen," said the old bird. "What is that sound?"

"It's too gentle for guns," said the young pheasants meditatively.

"Yes," said the old bird. "That's church bells. No one shoots on Sunday. They're going to play golf."

IX Responsibility

Once upon a time there was an ostrich who, though very ostrichy, was even more of an egoist. He thought only of himself. That foible is not confined to ostriches, but this particular fowl—and he was very particular—was notable for it. "Where do I come in?" was a question written all over him—from his ridiculous and inadequate head, down his long neck, on his plump fluffy body, right to his exceedingly flat and over-sized feet.

It was in Afric's burning sand—to be precise, at the Cape—that, on the approach of danger, the fowl in question secreted his self-centred head, and here from time to time his plumes were plucked from him for purposes of trade.

Now it happened that in London there was a theatre given up to a season of foreign opera, and, this theatre having been designed by one of those gifted geniuses so common among theatre architects, it followed that the balcony (into which, of course, neither the architect nor the manager for whom it was built had ever strayed) contained a number of seats from which no view of the stage was visible at all—unless one stood up, and then the people behind were deprived of the fraction of view that belonged to them, while to move one's head to one side or open a programme wide was also to cut the line of vision of others. This, of course, means nothing to architects or managers. The thought that jolly anticipatory parties of simple folk bent upon a happy evening may be depressed and dashed by a position suffering from such disabilities could not concern architects and managers, for some imagination would be needed to understand it.

It happened that on a certain very hot night in July a fat lady in one of the front seats not only moved about but fanned herself intermittently with a large fan.

Now and then one of the unfortunate seat-holders behind her remonstrated gently and politely, remarking on the privation her fan was causing to others, and each time the lady smiled and said she was very sorry and put the fan down; but in two minutes she was fluttering it again as hard as ever, and the stage was again blotted out.

She meant well, poor lady; but it was very hot, and how could she help it when her fan was made of that particular ostrich's feathers?

X Man's Limitations

Once upon a time there was a trout who lived in a stream much frequented by anglers. But though he was of some maturity and had in his time leapt at many flies, they had always been living insects and not the guileful work of man. Hence, although well informed on most matters, of the hard facts of fishing he knew only what he had been told by such of his friends as had been hooked and had escaped, and from watching the ancient dentist of his tribe at work in his surgery, extracting barbs from jaws. For, just as children stand at the smithy door watching the making of a horseshoe, so do the younger trout cluster round the dentist and observe him at his merciful task.

This trout was in his way a bit of a dandy, and one of his foibles was to be weighed and measured at regular intervals (as a careful man does at his Turkish bath), so that he might know how things stood with him. Fitness was, in fact, his fetish; hence, perhaps, his long immunity from such snares as half Alnwick exists to dangle before the eyes of undiscriminating and gluttonous fish.

But to each of us, however wise or cautious, a day of peril comes soon or late. It happened that on the very afternoon on which he had learned that he was eleven inches and a quarter long and turned the scale at twelve ounces, the trout met with a misadventure which not only was his first but likely to be his last. For seeing a particularly appetising-looking fly on the surface of the water, and being rather less carefully observant than usual, he took it at a gulp, and straightway was conscious of a sharp pain in his right cheek and of a steady strain on the same part of his person, pulling him upwards out of the stream.

Outraged and in agony, he dashed backwards and forwards, kicked and wriggled; but all in vain; and at last, worn out and ashamed, he lay still and allowed himself to be drawn quietly from the water in a net insinuated beneath him. In another moment he lay on the bank beneath the admiring and excited eyes of a man.

A pair of hands then seized him and the hook was extracted from his right cheek with very little tenderness.

It was at this moment that the trout's good fairy came to his aid, for the man in his eager delight placed him where the turf sloped. The trout saw the friendly stream just below, gathered his strength for a last couple of despairing struggles, and these starting him on the downward grade he had splashed into the water again before the angler realised his loss.

For a while the trout lay just where he sank, motionless, too exhausted to swim away, listening languidly to what was being said about him on the bank by the disappointed angler to a friend who had joined him. At length, having collected enough power, he glided to safety.

That evening, you may be sure, the trout had

plenty to tell his companions when, after their habit, they discussed the day's events in a little crowd. There were several absentees from the circle, and two or three fish who were present had swollen jaws where hooks had caught and broken away; while one actually had to move about and eat and talk with a foot of line proceeding from his mouth, attached to a hook which none of the efforts of the profession had been able to dislodge.

"But the thing that bothers me," said our trout, as he finished the recital of his adventures for the tenth time, "is men's curious want of precision. For while I was lying there in the water getting back my strength, I distinctly heard the fellow who had had me in his hands but had lost me, telling his friend that I was two feet four if I was an inch, and weighed within an ounce or two of three pounds."

XI "East, West, Home's Best"

Once upon a time there was a little girl who was taken to the Zoo by her father. Her father's tastes were wholly scientific: he paid several guineas a year for the privilege of forgetting to give away Sunday tickets; he could add F.Z.S. to his name if he liked; and when he went in he asked for a pen and wrote his name instead of paying a shilling like inferior folk. But the little girl was curiously unmoved by the world's strange fauna, whether elephants or water-beetles, and the result was that she followed listlessly and fatigued at her father's heels throughout the expedition, while with eager eyes he scrutinised this odd creature and that: from the very post-impressionist mandril, now no more, to the distant and incredible camelopards.

The little girl, I say, was listless and fatigued—for all but two minutes. For it chanced that as they walked in solemn procession through the house of the ostriches and the emus and various cassowaries named after their discoverers, they came to the Patagonian Cavy, and the little girl, loitering at his bars, uttered a gasp of delight, for there, all unconcerned and greedy, sat a tiny English mouse, eating grain.

The mouse looked at her with its brilliant eyes, and nibbled as though there were only two minutes of all time left for refreshment; and, secure in the knowledge of the dividing bars, it refused even to blink when she flicked her hand at it. She never noticed the Patagonian Cavy at all.

"What is it? What is it?" her father impatiently inquired.

"Hush!" she said. "Do come back and look at this darling little mouse."

"Pooh—a mouse!" said her father, and strode on, eager to reach the elusive apteryx.

"Well," said her mother when the little girl returned, "and what did you see that pleased you best?" and the little girl mentioned the mouse.

And what of the mouse? "You may call yourself a Patagonian Cavy," he remarked later in the evening, "but it doesn't follow that you're everybody. Did you notice a little girl with a blue bonnet this afternoon? Just after tea-time? The one that called her father back to have another look? Well, being a poor benighted Patagonian, you don't, of course, know what she said, but it wasn't what you think it was, oh dear no. It wasn't anything about you and your remarkable beauty. What she said was, 'Do come back and look at this darling little mouse,' which merely," the mouse concluded, "again illustrates an old contention of mine that good taste is not an adult monopoly."

XII Waste

Once upon a time there were three toadstools. They were not the fat brown ones like buns with custard underneath, or the rich crimson ones with white spots, or the delicate purple ones. They were merely small white ones, a good deal more like mushrooms than it was quite fair to make them.

They sprang up within a few inches of each other, and every moment added to their stature, and, as they grew, they discussed life in all its branches and planned for themselves distinguished careers. . . .

The eldest was not more than eighteen hours old, which is a good age for a toadstool, when an angry boy on his way home from the village school kicked him into smithereens for not being a mushroom—which is the toadstool's unpardonable sin.

The younger brothers, watching the tragedy, vowed to fulfil their destiny with better success than that, and forthwith they prepared a placard that ran as follows (in a form of words which was not perhaps strictly original):

> TO THE NOBILITY AND GENTRY OF TOADLAND.
>
> **YOU WANT THE BEST SEATS. WE HAVE THEM.**

Having placed this notice in a prominent position, they waited.

For some time nothing happened, and then an extremely portly and aristocratic toad, with eyes of burning amber and one of the most decorative waistcoats out of Bond Street, waddled towards the expectant brothers, read the advertisement, and sat heavily down on the nearer of them. I need hardly say that the stool was crushed to pieces beneath his weight, while the toad himself sustained, as the papers say, more than a few contusions, and was in a disgusting temper.

It was not long afterwards that a small girl, who had been sent out by her mother to pick mushrooms, added the surviving brother to her basket with a little cry of triumph. "What a beauty!" she said, and hurried home with the prize.

But her mother was very sharp about it. "Do you want us all in our graves?" she snapped, as she picked the toadstool up and flung it into the ash-bin.

"And not even the satisfaction of poisoning any one!" he murmured.

XIII Nature

Once upon a time there was a king who failed to please his subjects and was in consequence in instant peril. Hurriedly collecting together such treasures as he could, he and his young queen crossed the frontier one night with a few faithful retainers and settled in a secluded castle in a friendly country.

On the first wet day the young queen was missing. High and low the retainers searched for her, and at last she was discovered in the middle of an open space in the forest, holding up her face to the rain.

Horror-stricken, they hurried to her aid; but she waved them back.

"Do let me stay a little longer," she pleaded. "All my life I have longed to feel the rain and I was never allowed to. All my life there have been coaches and umbrellas."

And again the little queen held up her face to the drops.

XIV The Rule

Once upon a time there lived and flourished in a small city a worthy man. He was devoted to his native place; he loved its streets and stones, its strange odours, its smoke, its high rates, its indifferent water supply, its clubs and cafés and everything about it. Nothing could induce him to leave it even for the briefest period. In vain did the railway companies spread their Holiday Arrangements before his eyes; he returned with the more satisfaction to his favourite seat overlooking the central square.

And then one day the king of that country, who was full of capricious impulses, issued a decree that no one in this little city should ever leave it again.

And immediately the worthy man began to be consumed with a longing for travel.

XV The Uses of Criticism

Once upon a time there was an innkeeper who, strange to say, was unable to make both ends meet. Nothing that he tried was any use: he even placed in the windows a notice to the effect that his house was "under entirely new management," but that too was in vain. So in despair he consulted a wise woman.

"It is quite simple," she said, as she pocketed her fee. "You must change the name of your inn."

"But it has been 'The Golden Lion' for centuries," he replied.

"You must change the name," she said. "You

must call it 'The Eight Bells'; and you must have a row of seven bells as the sign."

"Seven?" he said; "but that's absurd. What will that do?"

"Go home and see," said the wise woman.

So he went home and did as she told him.

And straightway every wayfarer who was passing paused to count the bells, and then hurried into the inn to point out the mistake, each apparently believing himself to be the only one who had noticed it, and all wishing to refresh themselves for their trouble; motorists, observing the discrepancy as they flew by, stopped their chauffeurs, and, with the usual enormous difficulty, got them to go back; and the joke found its way into the guide-books.

The result was that the innkeeper waxed fat, lost his health and made his fortune.

XVI Joints in the Armour

Once upon a time there was a father of five who, living as he did in constant fear of their inquiring minds, took home with him a fat volume called *The Parents' Book,* because in the advertisements it claimed to answer children's questions by the thousand.

"Now, you little demons," he said genially that evening, "gather round and do your worst; your father's up to any trick. Ask me anything you like and I'll give you the answer·" and he opened *The Parents' Book*. "It is too much to hope, dear Eric," he added, turning to the eldest, "that there is nothing that you particularly want to know to-day?"

"Yes," Eric said with disconcerting quickness, "it is, father. What does 'Piccadilly' mean?"

Now this was something that the father had himself always wanted to know, so he turned up the index with some satisfaction and more confidence. But no "Piccadilly." Then he turned to "London" and was referred to page 491. "London is not only the largest but also the richest and busiest city in the world," it began. But nothing about Piccadilly at all!

Eric retired unsatisfied, and Cuthbert took the floor. "Please, father," he said, "what became of the wine after the Duke of Clarence was drowned in it?"

No "Clarence" in the index.

"I expect it was given to the poor," said Cuthbert philosophically, and with the lowest opinion of reference books he too retired.

"Now, Patricia?" the father said to his eldest girl. Patricia being a great reader he expected a literary poser. As it happened, he got it.

"What was the good news brought from Ghent to Aix?" she asked.

The index this time seemed more promising, for it gave—

Browning, Elizabeth Barrett . . . 551
—— Robert 552

but though the poem was mentioned nothing was said as to the very reasonable information desired.

Patricia therefore withdrew to make room for Horace, who merely asked who discovered that eggs had to be boiled. The father knew that it was useless to hope for light there, so he gave it up at once. "Arising out of that question," Horace therefore added (in his own juvenile paraphrase), "may I ask who first boiled a pot?" but the learned disquisition on "fire" provided by the volume did not go into that.

Things were getting very bad. Here were four of the little brood unanswered and the credit of literature was getting desperately thin.

"Now, Augusta," he said to the youngest, "can't you think of some problem that we—this volume and I—*can* solve for you?'

"Yes," she said with a suspicious wriggle. "Surely, father, more than two fleas got into the Ark, didn't they?"

XVII The Resolute Spirit

Once upon a time there was in a Suffolk village of South Highbolt a Tudor grange. It was richly timbered, with vine leaves carved on its barge-boards, and it had a great hall with a roof-tree springing from a cross-beam of massive stoutness, and a very beautiful pilastered gallery, and altogether it was just the house, although damp and insanitary, to send poetical travellers into raptures. But it had come upon evil days, and having been bought cheaply by a speculative London builder had been sold by him at an enormous profit to an American plutocrat, and was now being taken down with great care, every brick, stone, and beam numbered, to be re-erected in the American millionaire's estate on the banks of the Hudson, as a garden hostel for his guests, and a perpetual reminder of a country older and more romantic than his own.

It happened that, like most Tudor granges, this one was haunted, and had been ever since the year 1592, when a wealthy heir apparent, named Geoffrey, had been poisoned with a dish of toadstools by his spendthrift younger brother, more than anxious to upset the exasperating financial provisions of primogeniture, and their sister Alice had unconsciously partaken of the same dish. From that time onward Alice and Geoffrey, as well as could be managed in their disembodied state, had devoted themselves to the old home; and you may then imagine their dismay on seeing its component parts gradually being packed into a series of trucks, to be drawn to some distant spot by a traction-engine. To demolition pure and simple they were accustomed. Many were the neighbouring mansions, most of them also haunted, which they had seen pulled down, and not a few rebuilt; but it was a new experience to observe a house bodily removed they knew not whither, nor could they discover. In vain were other ghosts consulted;

none knew, not even the youngest. The point then was, what was to be done? for Geoffrey and Alice were divided in opinion as to their duty, Alice considering that her first allegiance was to the structure and its successive imprudent occupants, and Geoffrey that his was to the site.

"It is our family home," said Alice; "marry, we must go with it, no matter whither."

"Nay, sister," said Geoffrey, "that were foolish. We are Suffolk ghosts—more than Suffolk, South Highbolt ghosts—and here we ought to stay. Suppose it is going to London—how then? You are far too simple and countrified for the great city. The others would laugh at you."

"Let them," said Alice, "I care not."

"Wait till you hear them," said Geoffrey, "all sensitive as you are! Anyway, here I mean to stay."

"But how foolish!" said Alice; "for surely, Geoffrey, you would not haunt nothing? What use could that be? How can you make nothing creak? or blow out candles when there are none? or moan along passages that do not exist? or wring your hands in South Highbolt at casements that are elsewhere?"

"True," replied Geoffrey, "but I can carry on the mechanism of haunting just the same. I can gibber where the old home used to stand, as many another honest Suffolk ghost, aye, and Essex and Norfolk ghosts too, I wis, are doing at this moment. I belong to the village and shall stay here. I hate travel. No doubt to create anything like the sensation to which I have been accustomed will be difficult, but I can do my best. Even the poorest efforts, however, will be better than accompanying a traction-engine along a public road in broad day—verily a degrading occupation for the unlaid spirit of a fair lady."

"Circumstances alter cases," Alice replied. "I conceive my duty to be to yonder wood and stone. Nothing shall shake me. Wherever they go, there shall I go also."

"And I too," said Geoffrey, "am adamant. South Highbolt is my home and never will I desert it."

It therefore happened that when the time came for the road-train to leave, every vestige of the house being packed away, Alice took a tearful farewell of her brother and crept dismally into the last truck with a bibulous brakesman, and so broken was her spirit at leaving home, or such the completeness of his potations, that she caused him not a single tremor all the way to Harwich, where a vessel was waiting to convey the grange to America. Not until Alice grasped the fact that a sea voyage was before her, and took up her abode in the stuffy hold as near to the roof-tree as she could nestle, did her courage for the first time begin to fail, for she was a bad sailor; but once again duty triumphed. . . .

It was on the first night on which the re-erected Tudor grange was opened as a hostel for the millionaire's guests that Alice was placed in the delectable position of realising that the consciousness of having been virtuous is not always the only reward of a virtuous deed; for she had not waved her arms more than twice, nor uttered more than three blood-curdling shrieks, when Professor Uriah K. Bleeter, one of the most determined foes of the American Society of Psychical Research and all its works, sprang through his bedroom window to the ground below, taking with him the sash and some dozens of diamond panes.

And now the Tudor grange is even emptier than it had been for so long in England, and the millionaire who bought it lives entirely on his yacht.

XVIII In Extremis

Once upon a time a Nut lay dying. He was twenty-five. He had had a good time—too good—and the end was near.

There was no hope, but alleviation was possible. "Is there anything," he was asked, "that you would like?"

He was plucky and prepared for the worst.

"Yes," he said, "I'd like to know what I've spent since I was twenty. Could that be arranged?"

"Easily," they said.

"Good," he replied. "Then tell me what I've spent on my bally old stomach—on food."

"On food," they replied. "We find that you have spent on yourself an average of a pound a day for food. For five years that is, roughly, £1825."

"Roughly?" said the Nut.

"Yes. Counting one leap year, it would be £1826. But then you have entertained with some freedom, bringing the total to £3075."

"Yes," said the Nut. "And what about drinks?"

"We find," was the reply, "that on drinks your average has been three pounds a day, or about £5475 in all."

"Good heavens!" said the Nut. "What a noble thirst! And clothes?"

"The item of clothes comes to £940," they said.

"Only three figures!" said the Nut. "How did I come to save that odd £60, I wonder?"

"Not by any idea of economy," they replied. "Merely a want of time."

"And let's see," said the Nut, "what else does one spend money on? Oh yes, taxis. How much for taxis?"

"Your taxis," they said, "work out at seven shillings a day, or £639. 2s. 0d."

"And tips?" the Nut inquired.

"Tips," they said, "come to £456."

The Nut lay back exhausted, and oxygen was administered. He was very near the end.

"One thing more," he managed to ask. "What have I paid in cloak-room fees for my hat and stick?"

"Only £150," they said.

But it was enough: he fell back dead.

XIX Progress

Once upon a time there was a little boy who asked his father if Nero was a bad man.

"Thoroughly bad," said his father.

Once upon a time, many years later, there was another little boy who asked his father if Nero was a bad man.

"I don't know that one should exactly say that," replied his father: "we ought not to be quite so sweeping. But he certainly had his less felicitous moments."

XX Moses

Once upon a time there dwelt, in the city of Paris, in an appartement not very distant from the Étoile or Place of the Arc de Triomphe, two little boys. They were American boys, and they had a French governess. In addition to this they were twins, but that has nothing to do with Moses. I relate the fact merely to save you the trouble of visualising each little boy separately. All that you need do is to imagine one and then double him.

Well, after their lessons were done these two little boys used to go for a walk with their governess in the Champs Élysées, or the Parc Monceau, or even into the Bois itself, wherever, in fact, the long-legged children of Paris take the air; and no doubt as they walked they put a thousand

Ollendorffian questions to Mademoiselle, who had all her work cut out for her in answering, first on one side and then on the other. That also has nothing to do with the story, except in so far as it shows you the three together.

Well, on one morning in the spring one of the little boys saw something tiny struggling in the gutter, and, dragging the others to it, he found that it was a young bird very near its end. The bird had probably fluttered from the nest too soon, and nothing but the arrival of the twins saved its life.

"Voilà un moineau!" said Mademoiselle, "moineau" being the French nation's odd way of saying sparrow; and the little creature was picked up and carried tenderly home; and since sparrows do not fall from the heavens every day to add interest to the life of small American boys in Paris, this little bird had a royal time. A basket was converted into a cage for it and fitted with a perch, and food and drink were pressed upon it continually. It was indeed the basket that was the cause of the bird's name, for as one of the twins, who was a considerable Biblical scholar, very appositely remarked, "We ought to call it Moses because we took it out of the water and put it in a thing made of rushes." Moses thus gained his name and his place in the establishment; and every day he grew not only in vigour but in familiarity. After a little while he would hop on the twins' fingers; after that he proceeded to Mademoiselle's shoulder; and then he sat on the desk where the boys did their little lessons and played the very dickens with their assiduity.

In short Moses rapidly became the most important person in the house.

And then, after two or three weeks, the inevitable happened. Some one left a window open, and Moses, now an accomplished aviator, flew away. All befriended birds do this sooner or later, but rarely do they leave behind them such a state of grief and desolation as Moses did. The light of the twins' life was extinguished, and even Mademoiselle, who, being an instructor of youth, knew the world and had gathered fortitude, was conscious of a blank.

So far, I am aware, this narrative has not taxed credulity. But now comes the turning-point where you will require all your powers of belief. A week or so after their bereavement, as the twins and their governess were out for their walk, scanning, according to their new and perhaps only half-conscious habit, with eager glances every group of birds for their beloved renegade, one of them exclaimed, "Look, there's Moses!"

To most of us one sparrow is exactly like another, but this little boy's eye, trained by affection, did not err, for Moses it truly was. There he was, pecking away on the grass with three or four companions.

"Moses!" called the twins; "Moses!" called the governess, "Moses! Moses!"—moving a little nearer and nearer all the time. And after a few moments' indecision, to their intense rapture Moses flew up and settled in his old place on Mademoiselle's shoulder and very willingly allowed himself to be held and carried home again.

This is a free country (more or less) and any one is at liberty to disbelieve my story and even to add that I am an Ananias of peculiar ripeness, but the story is true none the less, and very pretty too, don't you think?

And could it, I have been wondering, ever have happened had it not been for M. Pol? You know M. Pol, of course. M. Pol is that engaging and not too dandiacal old gentleman who for years and years fed the sparrows, and chaffed them, and scolded them, in the gardens of the Tuileries. Whether or no he still carries on his gracious work I cannot say; he was looking very frail when last I saw him, a little before the war; but is it too much to hold that his influence still persists, in view of the extraordinary events which I have just related, and which, as I said before, are true? One must not claim too much for M. Pol or underrate the intelligence of Moses. None the less I feel strongly that, had it not been for M. Pol's many years of sympathetic intercourse with those gamins of the air, the Parisian sparrows, and all his success in building that most difficult of bridges —the one uniting bird and man—the deeds of Moses might never have come before the historian.

IN A NEW MEDIUM

THE OLD COUNTRY; OR, WRIT IN WAX

FOR most authors, and indeed all who confide themselves to prose and never dabble in words for music, the busy bee performs a large part of his labours in vain. In other words, they have no use for those preparations of wax with which gramophone records are made. But now and then even a writer of prose is susceptible to aberration, and it was during one such mood, not so long ago, that the idea came to me to put together some couplets which, when repeated by the gramophone with certain realistic accessories, might have the effect of reminding distant emigrants of the England that they have left, possibly fill them with home-sickness, and incidentally be of assistance to me in adding butter to bread.

At the first blush one might say that such a motive savoured if not of cupidity at any rate of inhumanity; but I believe that people derive more pleasure from a pensive melancholy, a brooding, lingering wistfulness, than from many positive delights: and it was this seductive nostalgia that my verses were designed to bring to them.

The suggestion came to me, suddenly, as I listened in a music hall to a French gentleman in evening dress whose special genius lay in the imitation of birds. Such was the fidelity with which he trilled forth the notes of the nightingale on the cold January evening on which I heard him, that he made the thought of June almost unbearable: and upon that pain of my own I resolved to try and erect an edifice of not disagreeable unhappiness in others.

Talking over the project with one who is behind the scenes in Edisonian mysteries, I obtained my first glimpses into the rules that govern the activities of the talking machine. Possibly these facts are commonplaces to the reader; but to me they were startling novelties. Each record, he told me, has to be of a definite length, of which two minutes is the extreme, and whatever words and effects I was aiming at must therefore be compressed into that space. This meant an instant modification of my scheme, for I had planned no more than enough material for one minute; and it was then that the skylark fluttered into the heavenly choir, and the catalogue of the country's charms, as you will shortly see, divided itself into day and evening.

The next thing that the expert told me was that one must not be too clever.

Here of course I bowed, murmuring something about impossibility.

By too clever, he went on, without paying any attention to my deprecation, he meant too literary. The gramophone public was not absurdly discriminating: the appeal being through the ear alone, and a swift one at that, there must be no ambiguity, no preciosity; each word must do its own work, and do it emphatically.

I agreed, and was conscious again of that feeling of respect which always comes upon me in the presence of one of those rare masterful beings who know what the public want.

"Why not," he went on, "complete the picture? Call the first part 'The Village,' and then provide a city pendant for the other side of the record, so that the town-dweller as well as the country-dweller may be *roped in?*" (The italics are his.)

"Why not indeed?" I replied.

"With city effects which will occur to you," he said.

"Of course," said I, and walked thoughtfully away, realising once more how dangerous a matter is impulse. Why had I ever embarked on this scheme? Why had I abandoned my old friend prose? Why was I flirting with science? . . .

None the less as I went on I found a certain amusement in writing verses for wax, and gradually "The Old Country" was finished—Part I. The Village, and Part II. The Town—and ready to be converted into magic.

To what extent gramophone recording rooms differ I cannot say; but the one in which "The Old Country" was prepared is on a top floor in the city of London, with large windows through which more than one of Wren's spires may be seen. In it, when I arrived, were gathered the orchestra, the conductor, the chief operator (in a long surgical coat), the elocutionist who was to deliver the lines into a metal funnel, the French gentleman with an aviary in his throat, my friend the expert, and a number of supernumeraries for London's cries and tumult—some of which indeed we could then hear by opening the window, but not loudly enough for our dramatic purpose.

Every one seemed composed and at peace with the world, except the elocutionist, who paced the floor muttering my poor verses over to himself in an agony that did me no credit; myself, who could not but be infected by his distress; and the French gentleman, who wandered disconsolately among the company, talking to no one, but occasionally refreshing his memory as to the differences of note between the two birds he was engaged to reproduce: certainly an important point to settle definitely before we began.

Of the gramophone itself nothing was visible, for the recording was done behind the partition. Penetrating thither, I found that it consists of nothing but a revolving disk of yellowish brown wax, into which a needle, vibrating to the elocutionist's voice and my wonderful poetry, was to plough furrows, throwing up a churning wake of gossamer shavings as it did so; these furrows, which are of every shade of depth, by Edisonian black art registering and subsequently giving forth again my exact syllables for all the world to hear. But how or why I shall never understand.

I have vague recollections of an explanatory lecture on the subject from the chief operator;

but science being a sealed book to me, I can pass none of its secrets on. The telephone and the telegraph, the Marconigraph and the automatic piano-player, will never be anything but the darkest enigmas; and almost before any of them comes, for marvellousness, the gramophone. But to the chief operator in his surgical coat its simplicity is a matter for laughter. So different are we all! Of such variety is human intelligence!

The three or four rehearsals, for time signals and so forth, being completed, we began. This was the procedure. First, absolute silence. Then the electric lamp on the operator's partition turning to red, the orchestra played a bar or so of "Home, Sweet Home," into which the elocutionist, who had now taken off not only his coat but his collar, for the better grappling with my muse, broke with the following lines:

O England, country of my heart's desire,
Land of the hedgerow and the village spire,
Land of thatched cottages and murmuring bees,
And wayside inns where one may take one's ease,
Of village greens where cricket may be played,
And fat old spaniels sleeping in the shade—
O homeland, far away across the main,
How would I love to see your face again!—
Your daisied meadows and your grassy hills,
Your primrose banks, your parks, your tinkling rills,
Your copses where the purple bluebells grow,
Your quiet lanes where lovers loiter so,
Your cottage-gardens with their wallflowers' scent,
Your swallows 'neath the eaves, your sweet content!
And 'mid the fleecy clouds that o'er you spread,
Listen, the skylark singing overhead . . .

It was here that my part of the production began, for the French gentleman, whose understanding of the whole matter seemed still exceedingly misty, in spite of rehearsals and instructions, had been placed wholly in my charge, and at the given moment I was to lead him as close as might be to the funnel, tap him, as agreed, on the shoulder, and thus let loose his skylark. Had there been no other bird, all would have been simple, but the presence also of the nightingale, in the same receptacle, was an embarrassment; and twice through nervousness he liberated the wrong chorister, and we had to begin again, while once I myself ruined an otherwise perfect record by exclaiming, when I thought it all over, "Bravo!" and slapping the French gentleman's back—this unfortunate remark attaching itself inseparably to the recitation.

It was not, I ought to say, exactly at the end of the verse that the skylark was to begin; but at the word "spread," the last line being spoken through the bird's notes. After that the blithe spirit had it all its own way for about ten seconds, when I tapped Monsieur sharply once more and drew him swiftly and silently away, while the reciter took his place at the funnel and with a sigh of satisfaction completed the first verse with these words:

That's the old country, that's the old home!
You never forget it wherever you roam.

Instantly the orchestra plunged into the opening of "The Swanee River," and again the reciter began, while I clung to the French gentleman in an agony, for the only expression on his countenance was one of determination to be a nightingale, whereas that on no account must he become until the words "they and I," almost at the end. With my arm firmly through his I awaited in a cold perspiration the cue. Here is the second verse:

I know an English village O so small!
Where every cottage has a whitewashed wall,
And every garden has a sweetbriar hedge,
And there's a cat on every window ledge.
And there's a cottage there with those within it
Whom I in fancy visit every minute.
O little village mine, so far away,
How would I love to visit you to-day!
To lift the latch and peep within the door
And join the happy company once more—
I think I'd try and catch them at their tea:
What a surprise for every one 'twould be!
How we would talk and laugh, maybe and cry,
Living our lost years over, they and I,
And then at dusk I'd seek the well-known lane
To hear the English nightingale again.

This time all went well. At "they and I" the nightingale broke in and continued until the concluding rounding-up couplet:

That's the old country, that's the old home!
You never can beat it wherever you roam.

So much for Part I. The Village. It was the end too of the French gentleman, at any rate for a while, and he went off to wet one or more of his many whistles, while the supernumeraries gathered together with designs on city illusion. One (a minute Osborne cadet, who appeared mysteriously from nowhere) carried a motor horn; another, a fire bell; another, a policeman's call; and a fourth, a wooden rattle which, when turned slowly, made a series of cracks resembling shots in a rifle saloon.

All being ready, we froze into silence and awaited the incarnadining of the lamp. Then one of the musicians struck Big Ben's chimes on a series of metal pipes, the orchestra followed with a bar or so of "Sally in our Alley," and the elocutionist plunged into Part II. The Town:

O London, once my home but now so far,
You shine before me brighter than a star!
By night I dream of you, by day I long
To be the humblest even of your throng:
Happy, however poor, however sore,
Merely because a Londoner once more.
Your sights, your sounds, your scents—I miss them all:
Your coloured buses racing down Whitehall;
The fruit stalls in the New Cut all aflare;
The Oval with its thousands gathered there;
The Thames at evening in a mist of blue;
Old Drury with a hundred yards of queue.
Your sausage shops, your roads of gleaming mud,
Your pea-soup fogs—they're in my very blood;
And there's no music to my ear so sweet
As all the noisy discord of the street.

At these words the reciter stepped aside and conceded the funnel to bus conductors shouting

"Higher up!" policemen ordering people to move on, newspaper boys with "All the Winners!" and costermongers noisily commending fruit; while in the background the Osborne cadet pinched the motor horn without mercy. At a signal, peace suddenly was restored, and

> That's my dear London, that's my old home,
> I'll never forget it wherever I roam,

said the elocutionist.

For the introductory bars of the second verse I had wanted "The Old Bull and Bush," but copyright difficulties intervening, we had to fall back upon "There is a tavern in the town," with which these words merged:

> And ah! the London pleasure parties too!—
> The steamboat up to Hampton Court or Kew;
> The walk among the deer in Richmond Park;
> The journey back, all jolly, in the dark!
> To Epping Forest up the Mile End Road,
> Passing the donkey barrows' merry load;
> Or nearer home, to Hampstead for a blow:
> To watch old London smouldering below;
> Between the Spaniards and Jack Straw's to pace
> And feel the northern breezes in one's face;
> Then at the Bull and Bush perhaps to dine
> And taste again their famous barley wine!
> Ah me! I wonder is it all the same?
> Is Easter Monday still the good old game?
> I hear it yet, though years have rolled away,
> The maddening medley of Bank Holiday.

Here came our greatest effect at realism. The band broke into a typical roundabout waltz, through which rifles snapped, whistles blew, cocoa-nut-shy men exhorted you to roll, bowl, or pitch, and a showman bellowed forth the importance of visiting a fat lady. And with the words:

That's my dear London, that's my true home,
I'll never forget it wherever I roam,

the record was complete.

What New Zealand and Australia, Johannesburg and the Yukon think of it, I have yet to learn. Nor has the butter begun to blossom on the bread. But it was great fun.

THE END